find that **job**

A SELF-HELP GUIDE FOR JOB SEEKERS IN IRELAND

find that job

AOIFE COONAGH with GERRY MULLINS

POOLBEG

Published 2009
by Poolbeg Books Ltd
123 Grange Hill, Baldoyle
Dublin 13, Ireland
E-mail: poolbeg@poolbeg.com

© Carr Communications 2009

1 3 5 7 9 10 8 6 4 2

A catalogue record for this book is available from the British Library.

ISBN 978-1-84223-423-5

Typeset by Patricia Hope in Georgia 10.2/14.5
Printed by
Colour Books Ltd, Baldoyle, Dublin, Ireland

www.poolbeg.com

About the Authors

Aoife Coonagh is Head of Career Development Services in Carr Communications. She is an experienced career consultant, HR professional and business trainer. Her expert advice and practical coaching support has enabled countless individuals to achieve their career goals with confidence and success. Aoife is a regular columnist, writing articles and features on career management and development issues for newspapers and professional/business publications.

Gerry Mullins was a Senior Communications Consultant at Carr Communications where he coached clients in job interview techniques, as well as media and presentation skills. He was previously a leading travel writer and is the author of two books on Irish history.

Introduction

Thank you for investing in your career and buying this book. I hope it helps you to secure your next job. You may be tempted to skip some chapters and reach for other chapters as you need them – the chapter on writing your CV or preparing for interviews, for example. You can certainly use the book in that way. However, I would encourage you to take an even more structured approach to your career planning, particularly in the current climate. Remember it is better to submit one well-targeted application than several poor ones. Getting a job is not a numbers game. With fewer opportunities, every CV, letter and effort towards a career move will carry even greater importance.

I have designed this book as a practical guide to help you plan and get the job you want *now*. It is like a workbook, with templates for you to complete, questions for you to consider and practical insights and experiences for you to learn from. Underline passages that you feel are especially important. Don't be precious with the book.

It will give you a structured approach to finding and getting a job. I use examples of real situations experienced by our clients. I've changed their names, but their experiences are real. Everything here has been learned through years of work, preparing people to excel and be successful at job interviews at all levels in countless organisations.

The knowledge gathered by my many colleagues has been invaluable, but I would especially like to thank Declan Farrell for writing sections, and Donal Cronin, Tony Hughes and Adrian Munnelly for their guidance. A special thank you to my co-author Gerry Mullins for encouraging me to write this book and co-ordinating the project. Thanks to Jennifer Kelleher for her expert editing skills.

Our practical approach to planning and managing career change has worked for thousands of people at various stages in their careers. I am confident it will work for you too. The very best of luck with your preparation and finding that job.

Aoife Coonagh,
Career Development Services,
Carr Communications,
Dublin, 2009.

For Larry, Lorcán and Ciara

Contents

Chapter 1

Evaluating Your Career

Whether you are starting your career, making a career change or considering your options in light of the current climate, the starting point should be the same. You need to take time to reflect on where you are now in your career, what you have learned, and then work out where you want to be. Once you know that, your job search and overall career path become far simpler. If this means you sit down for several days working out what your possible career could be, then it is time well spent. I have met many people in careers that didn't suit them; finding the right career sets them free.

Having worked with people at all levels of seniority from all kinds of organisations, I have observed something which you will know makes sense: nobody achieves full job satisfaction doing a job that they don't like.

Taking the time to reflect, working out what type of career or work you're looking for and planning the steps to find it should give you a better chance of finding what is right for you.

This section of the book is about helping you understand what it is you might excel at. After working through this chapter, you will know how to approach the following:

- Planning your Career Move
- Understanding your Achievements
- Auditing your Skills and Competencies
- Working out your Motivations, Interests and Values
- Where do you want to be?
- A Balancing Act – Work/Life Balance

Planning your Career Move – Where are you Now?

The career planning process is a journey that involves a number of simple steps. The questions in this section are designed to help you to think objectively about yourself – and to review and understand your achievements, personal strengths and skills – to help you make better career choices. Armed with this self-insight and knowledge you will be better able to clarify your future goals.

This is an opportunity to ask yourself questions you may have never asked yourself in the past, to help clarify where you are on your career path.

Using the following template, track your personal Life and Career path, listing significant milestones and dates since you left school. List the corresponding jobs you did and any courses you took. Depending on where you are in your career you may be summarising and grouping roles from twenty years ago – or making your four months on a J1 Visa in New York in second year in UCD sound like you ran the trading floor in ABC stock exchange!

Life and Career Path Template

Start by getting it all down onto paper for now as follows:

Date	Milestone	Important Details
1996	*Started college – UCD*	*BA Economics and Politics Got a first in exams*
Summer 1997	*J1 Visa – worked in New York office*	*Admin in accountancy 4 months*
1997	*Part-time job through college*	*PR work*
Summer 1998	*Summer placement in local AIB branch*	
1999	*Graduation*	*First class honours*
Summer 1999	*Internship in ABC Financial*	
Jan 2000	*Graduate Programme ABC Financial* *9 month placements in 4 departments*	*Banking, Insurance, Commercial,* *Lending and Foreign exchange*
Apr 2001	*Started accountancy course*	
Sept 2003	*Appointed Senior Bank official*	*Projects role in lending section*
	And so on . . .	

Below is a blank Life and Career Path Template for you to fill in.

Date	Milestone	Important Details

This next section will help you to review your career; the roles and highlights. You'll need to figure out what's important for the next job, and be able to answer some key questions:

- What have I achieved to date?
- What skills do I have?
- What strengths do I have?
- What work do I like or get a buzz from?
- What areas interest me?
- What's my ideal job?

It will be crucial to use this information on your CV and cover letter to highlight your suitability for particular roles and sell your skills. Likewise at interviews, you'll need to be comfortable explaining your achievements and linking them to the role you're seeking. So . . .

Understanding your Achievements

This is the one question candidates tell me they hate at interview; but it is the one question interviewers love to ask and probe. *Why was X actually an achievement? And so what exactly did you do? And why was that important?*

3

Most candidates are uncomfortable talking about their achievements – they feel it is in some way boastful or immodest. However, your achievements can tell a lot about your skills, your motivation and ability to finish projects – all things an interviewer will want to know more about. They are interested in understanding how you contributed in your previous roles and they will use this as an indicator of how you might contribute in their job role.

Identifying your Achievements
Using your Life and Career Path page, reflect on each item at each stage. Reflect on:

- the various job roles you've held
- the courses you've done
- personal milestones
- any extra roles you've held or involvement with committees or clubs.

Really begin to think about your personal accomplishments and professional achievements or projects over your life and your career path to date. Start listing these achievements and projects in column 1 on the Achievements Matrix on page 5.

Your Life and Career Path page and the Achievements Matrix will provide you with the material you need to compile your new CV. If the achievements and accomplishments you've listed are not already on your CV, we'll make sure to include them when we get to the next chapter.

Your role, input and contribution
You also need to highlight your personal contribution and role in these achievements and projects. I frequently meet job applicants who merely list that they worked on a particular project, believing that the interviewer will be able to infer from that what he or she needs to know. They won't. You need to work it out. On the matrix, fill in Column 2, expanding on your role and personal contribution, highlighting any key inputs you made to achieve the results you did.

Result and outcome
You should also record the result or outcome of each of your achievements. List these in Column 3. Think about how this result or outcome contributed

to your success in your company or college course. Sometimes the outcome may have been unsuccessful, even if your input was strong. That's okay. We often learn more from failed projects than successful ones. The important thing to remember is that you need to know what you'd do differently, and be able to describe what you learned from the experience.

Why is this important to me?

You need to be able to describe why your achievements and accomplishments are important to you. Sometimes it will have been an important lesson, other times an important boost to your confidence. In addition, knowing why an achievement is important to you can help you to explain to an interviewer what motivated you to succeed. Reflecting on this can also help to uncover personal values that influenced you and your decisions. Understanding these can be useful in helping you identify suitable roles.

Achievements Matrix

What have you achieved to date?

My Key Achievements Matrix

Achievement and Accomplishment	My Role My Input My Contribution	Result/ Outcome	Why important to me?
Example: *Transformed unproductive storage space into shelf display area, yielding increased commercial area.*	*My idea; I secured the funding and led the renovation.*	*More attractive retail space. Increased sales by 15%. Project expected to break even within 18 months.*	*Showed I could conceive a project, get buy-in, and see it through to a successful completion.*

Donal Cronin, Director of Training and Career Coach with Carr Communications, explains the benefits of career planning:

> Career planning is not just a single exercise. It's about stepping back and understanding your past career so you can be more effective in your future one. What you're trying to do is chart a career path, showing how one job has led to another and how your experience has broadened each time. It's also about helping you become comfortable explaining your career path to other people (the interview panel).
>
> So, even if it might look at first like you've been job-hopping, you look for the common thread, and link that to the job you're applying for. This means that when you face an interview panel, it becomes easy to explain that you didn't meander around, and that you made a difference every place you went.
>
> I get people to search through their achievements, pull out the details and explain them to a potential employer.

Auditing Your Skills

This section encourages you to tease out what you are good at and to list examples that you can use in an interview. Remember, employers are results-focused; they will want to employ you if you have the skills they are looking for. However, you will need to convince them that you have used these skills effectively in the past. Just because you've been a manager, or dealt with customers for twenty years, doesn't prove you were a good manager, or were able to deal effectively with customers. The interview board will need evidence and concrete examples that clearly demonstrates how you used your management or customer service skills effectively. So if these skills are important in the career you are considering, then add achievements where you demonstrated these skills to your Achievement Matrix.

Transferable Skills Audit

Employers are looking for people who bring a range of people and communications skills to a role, in addition to any specialist technical or business skills required.

Broadly speaking, employers are looking for employees who will

1. do the job well and **deliver the results** expected
2. work well with others and **develop relationships** with colleagues and clients

3. **communicate** clearly in writing and face to face
4. **manage** themselves and lead others if required
5. bring **personal qualities** such as motivation and loyalty
6. have the relevant **technical specialist skills** or **business skills**

To ensure you meet the criteria above, certain skills are required for most job roles. I have identified the most important of these skills, which are your transferable skills. I have created a questionnaire or Transferable Skills Audit for you to consider your own skills and assess if you have what employers are looking for under each heading.

This is not an exhaustive list and you should scrutinise the job descriptions to ensure you know the main skills required for the particular role you are going for.

As you work through the skills below, reflect on your own skill level and score yourself out of ten for each skill, and the sub-skills beneath. This will be useful in helping you identify possible strengths and development areas for yourself. If you trained professionally or have worked in a particular industry for some time you should have gained specific skills relevant to that industry. You need to be crystal clear what those specialist skills are. Use column 4 to list any additional technical or specialist skills you possess that are most relevant in your industry, e.g. research, health and safety, etc.

Transferable Skills Audit

1. **Delivering Results**
   - Organisation and Time Management
   - Budget and Resource Management
   - Problem Solving and Decision Making
   - Continuous Improvement

2. **People and Interpersonal Skills**
   - Interpersonal Skills
   - Customer Focus
   - Team-working
   - Networking and Relationships

3. Communication Skills
- Verbal Communication
- Written Communication
- Influencing and Negotiating
- Chairing and Facilitating Meetings

4. Management and Leadership Skills
- Leadership
- Managing Self
- Managing Others
- Change and Innovation

5. Personal qualities
- Achievement Focus
- Commitment
- Self-confidence
- Initiative

6. Technical, Specialist and Business Skills
- Technical skills
- Business/industry skills
- Commercial/Business Acumen
- Additional Technical or Specialist Skills

1. Delivering Results

Organisation and Time Management	Budget and Resource Management	Problem Solving and Decision Making	Continuous Improvement
Plans effectively	Understands finance	Analyses complex situations	Improves service delivery
Prioritises tasks	Budget management	Identifies options	Researches best practice
Monitors progress	Allocation of resources	Creates solutions	Leads change initiatives
Task focused	Tackles inefficiencies	Takes decisions	Acts on feedback
Meets deadlines	Initiates cost saving measures	Practical and pragmatic	Responds to new challenges

2. People and Interpersonal Skills

Interpersonal Skills	Customer Focus	Team-Working	Networking and Relationships
Diplomatic and tolerant	Approachable and professional	Contributor to the team	Establishes key contacts
Assertive with others	Anticipates needs	Listener with team mates	Manages stakeholder relationships
Understands others	Goes the extra mile to deliver	Supports the team	Respected and trusted
Effectively relates at all levels	Champion for organisation	Facilitates co-operation	Partnership approaches to business
		Delivers results	

3. Communication Skills

Verbal Communication	Written Communication	Influencing and Negotiating	Chairing and Facilitating Meetings
Clear communicator	Presents clear written documents	Presents clear case	Clarifies objectives
Questions	Professional layout and presentation	Gains commitment	Creates agenda
Presents confidently	Communicates messages clearly	Confronts issues professionally	Facilitates active participation
Achieves understanding	Uses clear simple English	Achieves win-win	Facilitates decision making
Focuses on audience			Agrees actions in next steps

4. Management and Leadership Skills

Leadership	Managing Self	Managing Others	Change and Innovation
Strategic thinker	Sets goals	Clarifies roles	Forward thinker
Visionary	Delivers results	Offers feedback	Enjoys change
Sets example	Develops new skills	Provides support	Suggests ideas
Provides direction for others	Sets standards	Coaches and develops others	Innovative and creative thinker
Motivates the team	Seeks feedback	Manages performance	Encourages others to challenge status quo
Decision maker			Takes calculated risks

5. Personal qualities

Achievement Focus	Commitment	Self-confidence	Initiative
Sets Challenges	Actively shows loyalty	Self-assured	Creative
Proactive Self-starter	Acts as an exemplar	Handles setbacks	Forward thinker
Opportunistic	Speaks positively about organisation	Confident decision maker	Intuitive
Motivated	Goes the extra mile	Maturity	Self-starter
		Tenacity	Innovative
		Drive	Action planner

6. Technical, Specialist and Business Skills

Technical Skills	Business / Industry Skills	Commercial / Business Acumen	Additional Technical / Specialist Skills
Specialist knowledge or skills	Professional skills	Strategic planner	
PC/IT skills	Industry specific skills	Forward thinker	
Language skills	Understanding of their business plan	Functional skills – finance, IT, HR, etc.	
Industry systems or packages		Entrepreneurial	
		Risk taker	

Now go back with a highlighter and identify those skills you most enjoy or get most job satisfaction out of using. Rank your strongest skills and identify any priority development areas based on the scores above. Did you use any of these skills to deliver your achievements in your Achievements Matrix? My guess is that you did.

Identify any skills you'd like to or need to develop. Consider a plan to do something about them. And remember, always start with achievable steps; otherwise you might become overwhelmed.

In addition to knowing the skills that are important to the organisation, you need to understand the level of skill they are looking for. Be aware of the **"step-up"** that may be required in some positions. For instance, if you are applying to move from team member to a team leader role, you'll need to work out how you'll manage the increased responsibility, and at interview prove you have skills required at the appropriate level.

On your CV and cover letter, and at interview, employers will be looking for how you effectively used and demonstrated these skills in the past.

My Skills and Strengths Chart

My Strongest Skills	Those I most enjoy
1.	
2.	
3.	
4.	
5.	
6.	
7.	
8.	
9.	
10.	

My Development Areas

1.

2.

3.

4.

5.

6.

7.

8.

9.

10.

One of our clients, Alan, used this approach to identify his main skills, particularly those that were transferable. He then targeted jobs where they would apply, thus enhancing his career and job satisfaction, because he's now using skills he enjoys.

I worked for a heavy engineering company, mostly in sales and marketing, and briefly in the manufacturing area. I wanted to move somewhere else in my career, but didn't know where.

I got help with my CV and career planning advice. We teased out my career achievements, and condensed my skills down to a list of seven. It soon became much clearer where my skills and interests lay.

I didn't realise it before, but it seemed I had strong management, operational and people management skills. I decided that I would like to work in the airline industry, even though I hadn't worked there before and it would pose a challenge to justify the move to any prospective employer.

However, because I was now sure of my strengths and interests, I was able to show how they were transferable to my target job. I had the confidence to justify my decision to make the change at the interview. And I succeeded.

Understanding Your Motivation, Interests and Values

What Motivates You?

You will only achieve real job satisfaction if you are motivated by the work you do. Many people skip over this important factor in their bid to get into the job market or to get a job on a higher salary. This is short-term planning, and rarely yields job satisfaction in the longer term.

Instead, you should try to understand what motivates you. For example, if helping people matters to you, then you should consider roles that give you the opportunity to do that. If you don't enjoy roles that put you in constant contact with people, then a role in sales, for example, may not be ideal.

Likewise, you should be aware of your values: if you feel strongly about protecting the environment, you should seek out organisations that have strong values in this area.

You will need to ask yourself what you have liked and disliked in your roles to date. Or, to put it another way, what has motivated you and what has de-motivated you in your previous jobs. Jot down the aspects you've enjoyed most in the various roles in your career, and those you'd like to change. These will be important considerations when deciding on whether to apply for new roles at the outset.

WHAT MOTIVATES ME?

Best things/enjoy most

Example:

Busy environment/targets/no slackers

Things I'd like to change or that de-motivated me

Example:

Lack of autonomy

Meetings/Reviews/Committees

What are your interests?

Reflecting on the things that interest you outside of work can also become a stimulus for possible areas of work. Think about your hobbies, extra-curricular activities and any other areas such as professional committees you are interested or involved in.

CURRENT AREAS OF INTEREST

Interests

Art

Environmental issues

Sport

Cooking

Areas of interest (above) where I would like to explore further careers possibilities e.g. related industries/fields of work.

Possible work in environmental roles

Set up art classes at weekend

Think about possible career opportunities in the areas of interest. Depending on what stage you are at in your career, different options will be open to you. Many of my clients have made career changes into an area that was previously a hobby for them. Here's one example:

> David, a legal professional, wanted to get out of the legal field. He loved writing, had published a few human interest pieces and wanted to do more. He's now writing human interest pieces for a number of papers and legal publications – using his legal expertise to explain court findings and making legal topics accessible to you and me.

You may also be able to draw on your extra-curricular activities to demonstrate skills that may be useful in the job. For example, if you've been effective as chairperson of your local school's board of management, this will show that you have chairing and leading abilities, even if your current job role doesn't reflect this.

Understanding your Values

Understanding your own values is very important, because if you have very strongly held beliefs and values, then some industries and organisational cultures may not suit you. And you most definitely won't get job satisfaction.

Think about your personal values and why they are important to you. Know the ones you won't compromise on in your search for a new role. When your personal values match those of the organisation you work for, you will achieve more job satisfaction.

My Personal Values

Personal

Honesty

Openness

Integrity

Relationships
Trust
Open

Social
Enjoy active social life

Community
*Want to give back to community (could be suited to
volunteer organisation)*

Creativity
*Enjoy coming up with new ideas and designing solutions to
solve problems*

Other
Green Issues

The Balancing Act – Work/Life Balance

This wheel of life (adapted from the Buddhist Dharma philosophy) is a simple tool designed to help you assess your level of satisfaction with different areas or aspects of your life. By scoring each aspect honestly, you should quickly see whether you are achieving work/life balance. You may need to set some goals to improve things if necessary.

Identify the areas in your life or aspects of your life that are important to you – e.g. family, education, work, etc. – and assign to a slice of the pie on the wheel of life below. I have labelled the wheel with the most common aspects. Now, reflect on your overall level of satisfaction with each aspect of your life and score your current level of satisfaction out of ten. Plot your score for each area on the wheel and join them up. This is your present position.

Now consider where you want to be in two or three years' time. Plot these scores on the wheel. Make sure to use different coloured pens for current and goal scores. Now join all the goal scores, so your wheel of life may look like the example on page 17.

For example, if you are fresh out of college and not keen on more courses for a while, you might score yourself a five in the "Learning and Education" section today. However, suppose in a few years you'd like to do more studies, possibly a Masters; so your goal score might be eight or nine in four or five years' time.

The next step is to consider how you will bridge any gaps between the two scores, and these steps should ideally become your action plan for the future.

Next, highlight the areas that are a priority for you right now. There should be a balance across all of the areas of importance in your life. List the ones you want to improve immediately and start taking action.

Use the Action Planning sheet on page 18 to help you plan your life and career goals.

The Wheel of Life

Where Do I Want To Be?

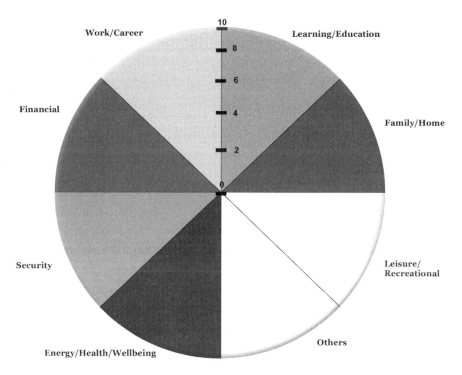

Rate your level of satisfaction with each area of your life at present.

Now highlight areas where you want to improve and take action.

Remember, work is about doing ABC to achieve XYZ.

My Action Plan

What steps do you need to take to move from where you are now to where you want to be? List the things you need to do to progress your career plan. Put dates against these actions. Identify who can help you. Track your progress.

My Action Plan

Next Steps and Actions	Target date	Help required	Progress

Having stepped back and reviewed your career you should now have a much better insight into your skills; particularly ones you are good at and have used successfully in the past. You will also be clearer on the aspects of previous job roles that motivated and interested you most.

Choosing career options where these skills and preferences are met by the role will result in you achieving job satisfaction.

Chapter 2

Considering Your Options

This chapter encourages you to think about your preferences at work. What type of roles are you best suited to? What type of cultures or environments do you enjoy most? Are you someone who needs a high degree of autonomy or do you require a team environment to keep you motivated?

Once you are clear on the type of organisational environment and team structures that work best for you, you should actively seek roles that have these characteristics. This increases your chances of finding a job that you'll enjoy and succeed at.

Think back over the various job roles you have held and list the characteristics of these roles that most suited you. Use the following headings as a guide.

In this chapter I will help you to consider the options available to you and to understand:

- Work Preferences
- Ideal job roles and sectors
- What you have to offer

Work Preferences

What is my preferred style of working?

> ## Relationships
>
> – With my manager
>
> – With colleagues
>
> – Individual or team

Work Environment

– Organisation culture

– Values

– Goals

– Recognition

– Growth and development

– Purpose

– Autonomy/control

Describing Your Ideal Job

What does your ideal job look like? What are its components – your "wish list"? Many clients I work with find that their ideal or dream job is not in their current field. Often they find that it's in a field related to their broader areas of interest and the tasks and responsibilities provide an opportunity for them to use their strongest skills.

Reflect on your strengths, skills and personal achievements. Think about your interests and work style or preferences. A clearer picture of the characteristics of your ideal job should now be emerging.

Key components of my ideal job

For example

1. *Helping or teaching people*
2. *Team leader or supervisory role*
3. *Small organisation with clear mission and explicit values and delivery in past*
4. *Opportunity to use my counselling and psychology training*
5. *Salary expectations of €xx,000*
6.
7.
8.
9.
10. *Near where I live*

Go back now and highlight those components of your ideal job that you will not compromise on. Know the ones that would be nice to have but aren't necessary for you to achieve job satisfaction. List possible job roles or fields of work that interest you most *and* meet the above criteria.

Preferred job options and fields of interest

1

2

3

4

5

Considering Options

The following section is designed to help you "think outside the box" and broaden your horizons when considering potential roles.

For example, if your ideal role is a sales role in the pharmaceutical sector, jot this down in the centre of the diagram.

Now think about similar roles in the sales area *and* in the pharmaceutical sector or related sectors, such as medical devices. You should also consider roles in slightly different but **related fields** – a client management or customer service role may have common elements that you would enjoy.

Now consider other sales roles in completely **different fields**. If you were successful at selling medical devices, you'll probably be good at selling similar products but in a different industry, perhaps selling engineering parts or electronic devices. Don't limit your scope at this stage.

Don't forget to include possible job roles in **other industries** and sectors you identified in the interests section on page 21. For instance, if you are interested in environmental issues, and know enough about it to branch into that area, you could try selling environmental products. Now you'd be using your transferable skills effectively and doing something you believe in and value.

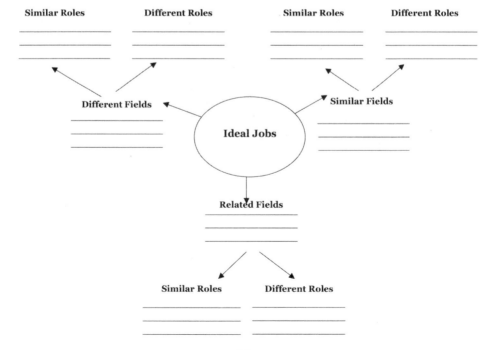

Depending on where you are on your career path, the following career options will be more or less important. Bearing in mind the goals that emerged from the Wheel of Life exercise in the last chapter, you may want to opt for a new way of working. Rather than going for a nine-to-five role, you may prefer to take part-time work and study as well, or even consider self-employment.

Examining Job Options

Consider the main options and job roles from the previous exercise that meet the criteria of your ideal role. Now start to research these roles – look for sample job descriptions on the internet to see exactly what they entail. Find out as much as you can so you can consider the following questions and decide if this is the type of role for you. Ask yourself the same set of questions for all of the possible roles you have identified.

Job Role 1

	Title_____
1. Why does this appeal to me? What are the benefits?	
2. Are there any risks or concerns? e.g. financial or personal	
3. How can I overcome these?	
4. How will I equip myself for the new organisation or field?	
5. What research do I need to do?	
6. Who can help me?	
7. Do I need any additional skills?	
8. How can I develop these?	
9. Where will I find these roles?	
10. What do I need to do to make it happen? Next steps . . .	

What I have to offer – Summary

Here is a useful way for you to summarise your achievements, skills, strengths and preferred options, as I have highlighted in Chapter 1 and in this chapter. Ideally, you should complete it before writing your CV, and if you have written one already, it should inform a fresh version of it. By completing this section, you will also be preparing for many of the questions you are likely to be asked at interview. The difference now is that you should be much clearer on what you have to offer and what your fit and match is for the role in question.

What I have to offer

My Key Achievements *See chart on page 5*	1. 2. 3. 4. 5. 6.
My Skills and Strengths *(My strongest skills and ones I enjoy the most)* *See chart on page 12*	1. 2. 3. 4. 5. 6.
Preferred job options and fields of interest *See chart on page 21*	1. 2. 3. 4. 5. 6.
My fit and match for the role	1. 2. 3. 4. 5. 6.

Chapter 3

Writing a Professional CV and Cover Letter

In the jobs market, the first impression is made by your CV, cover letter and/or your application form. Your application needs to provide critical evidence that you have the required skills, experience, knowledge, abilities and personal qualities to do the job well. And if your letter can stand out from the others then that also helps.

This part of the book is designed to help you do just that. You will learn how to write an honest CV that summarises what you bring to the job. Your CV will reflect the skills and achievements discussed in earlier chapters and will be clearly focused on the job role in question. I will take you through:

- Writing your CV
- Main Sections on a CV
- CV Dos and Don'ts
- Sample CVs
- The Executive CV
- Europass CV
- Key Components of a Cover Letter
- Sample Cover Letter
- Preparing Application Forms

Writing your CV

Having coached so many people over the years who are going for job interviews, I'm sometimes amazed when I read the description of the role they're going for and then read their CV. Often there is very little overlap, and they've made little or no attempt at linking the two. The good CVs, on the other hand, stand out from the rest of the pile because they have clearly tried to establish links. These CVs are more than just a list of dates and headings. In them, people attempt to:

✔ Show they can do the job in question

✔ Demonstrate and confirm how well they did previous jobs

✔ Indicate enthusiasm about the new role.

They do enough, in other words, to get called for interview.

An effective CV should highlight the features that make you an interesting candidate for this role and the benefits you might bring to your prospective employer. Your CV should:

✔ Reflect what the employer is looking for

✔ Clearly identify the relevant key skills you have

You need to consider your skills carefully and clearly identify:

✔ What skills or experiences make you stand out?

✔ What evidence backs this up?

✔ What skills do you have that are transferable to this company?

Refer to the Transferable Skills Audit on page 7 to help you identify the skills you need to outline on your CV. Employers will screen applicants on the basis of their CV and may take less than a minute to scan your CV. So make sure everything on your CV is explicitly relevant to the role.

There is no one layout or style that is the "right" layout for a CV. Ensure it is clearly laid out and easy to read, with the most important information at the top.

No matter what format or style you settle on, there are some key components and sections you should include:

• Personal Details

• Profile

• Education and Qualifications

- Employment History
- Interests
- Referees

Main Sections on a CV

Personal Details

This is simply your name, address and contact details, including your personal phone number (not that of your current employer) and a personal email address. Make sure that your personal email address looks professional, i.e. not containing a nickname or joke that may have seemed funny when you set it up, but wouldn't amuse a prospective employer. You do not need to include your marital status, family circumstances, race or religious beliefs in this section.

Profile

This is also referred to as Career Profile, Objective, Personal Profile or Skills Profile. It is a short statement about you and what you have to offer the employer. It is an executive summary or an overview of your experience and track record. A skills profile should outline your particular skills and strengths for the role.

You need to imagine the employer reading this and deciding on the strength of this statement whether or not to keep reading. In the profile, you give a summary of what you have to offer, keeping in mind what the employer wants and needs.

When writing your profile you might find it useful to ask yourself: "If the recruiter stopped reading my CV at this point, would they think I was right for the role?"

A profile is particularly important for executives and senior people who have had long and varied careers. For more information on this, see "The Executive CV" section on page 43.

Education and Qualifications

Include all professional qualifications achieved, starting with the most recent. You may wish to put an additional heading "Continuing Professional

Development" or "Other Training and Development" to include other work-related courses such as presentation skills, team leadership or health and safety training.

Employment History

Your most recent role will usually be the most relevant to the job for which you are now applying. So this should be the most detailed and come first, followed by your previous roles in reverse chronological order.

For each role include the following: the company, your role, dates from/to, and your achievements and results delivered in the job.

You can give a two- or three-sentence introduction to describe your role, give an overview of where it fits in the organisation and the level of responsibility.

For example: *Reporting to Director of X, with a team of five direct reports, managing a unit of 30 staff, controlling €x budget having Y units of sales targets.*

If your organisation is not well known, you might include a few sentences describing the organisation. Then, rather than listing six or eight bland, generic responsibilities, (which don't tell us how well you carried out these responsibilities), summarise your areas of responsibility using achievement statements. These should give a clear sense of how well you delivered in these areas; e.g. *"Grew sales from X to Y"*. Use bullet points so that they stand out.

Interests

Only include this section if you have extra-curricular interests that are relevant to the role or demonstrate skills that will be useful. Include non-work-related achievements in this section; for example: membership of a sports team, fundraising, and any community work.

Referees

It is not necessary to put down names and contact details or your referees here. Just insert the line "Available on request", and they can be given at a later stage. This means that when you do get called for the interview you can select the most relevant people, ring them, remind them of the role you're going for and send them the CV you sent to the employer.

CV Dos and Don'ts

Length

✔ A CV should be two or three pages long – unless it is in a specialised field such as medicine, which might require up to a dozen pages to list research and publications.

✔ Remember, the recruiter is getting hundreds of CVs; they will be instantly turned off by a ten-page CV.

✔ An employer wants to find the information quickly. If they have to search for it there is a strong chance they will give up after page two.

Correct Spelling

If an employer gets a CV with spelling mistakes or typos, they can only conclude:

✔ You cannot spell

✔ You are lazy

✔ You are inattentive to detail

It is not enough to run the CV through the spellcheck – this will not catch all typos. You must proofread it. It is difficult to proofread your own work successfully, so you should get someone else to look over it as well.

Beware of American spellings, unless you are applying to a company in North America. Words such as "organized", "recognized" and "organization" should be changed to their Irish/UK version ("organised", "recognised" and "organisation"). Ideally, set "Language" to "English (Ireland)", or "English (UK)" to avoid errors.

Short Sentences and Paragraphs

✔ Your CV should be as easy to read as possible for the employer. Long sentences can be complicated and difficult to read, whereas short sentences can be skimmed quickly. Shorter sentences have power.

✔ Keep your paragraphs short too. Instead of a big block of text, have a couple of lines followed by bullet points.

Never lie on a CV

- ✔ This can be as simple as saying you like reading, when you don't. In the interview you might be asked about the last book you read, and instantly lose credibility as you grasp for book titles.

- ✔ If you fail the credibility test in one part of your CV, the employer will begin to question the truth of the whole CV and a job offer will be unlikely.

- ✔ If you lie and apparently "get away with it" and get the job, there could be strong grounds for dismissal if the employer were to find out at a later date.

Font

- ✔ Choose a simple, well-recognised font that is easy to read. A serif font has what look like little feet and peaked caps on its letters. This is easier to read on the printed page than a sans-serif font (one without the little feet). So choose a serif font such as Times New Roman or Georgia instead of a sans-serif one such as Tahoma or Arial.

- ✔ Some organisations may specify the font you must use because they scan all CVs.

Heading Styles

- ✔ Use bold or increase the font size for headings. Do not use underline or all capitals as they are harder to read.

- ✔ If you like to use capital letters for headings use the "small caps" feature which gives the effect of upper and lower case i.e. HEADING STYLES.

Paper or Soft Copy?

- ✔ If you are posting your CV it should be printed out on good quality white standard A4 paper as some photocopy paper may be a bit flimsy.

- ✔ Use a good quality A4 envelope.

✔ When emailing your CV save it and your cover letter together as a PDF document before sending them. This avoids any complications with different versions of Word, which can give a slightly different version of a font and could cause problems with spacing. So what might print out the far end has far from the desired effect.

Golden Rules

✔ Use positive language, with action verbs e.g. _Delivered_ sales training to all new staff.

✔ Include results and achievements; e.g "resulting in an increase in overall sales of 10%".

✔ Do not include photographs, copies of references or qualifications, unless requested.

✔ Leave plenty of white space; no clutter or long paragraphs.

✔ Make sure your layout is clear and consistent – don't use lots of different fonts and formatting styles.

✔ Justify left only (i.e. align your text to the left-side margin). If you use full justification (left- and right-side margins) your sentences will be stretched across the page, causing uneven spacing between words.

✔ Make sure your headings, subheadings and bullet points are consistent in style and size.

✔ Remember, save your CV as a PDF to ensure the formatting is kept when you email it to a prospective employer.

Sample CVs

On the following pages are some sample CVs. The first three are slightly different versions of a CV for the same person and are presented in different ways to show alternative design styles and layouts. I have kept the first one to one page for illustration purposes and I have made suggestions and comments to highlight additional changes that could be made to enhance each of them.

Mark O'Reilly

5 Northumberland Road,
Ballsbridge,
Dublin 4.

086 1234567 / mark@gmail.com

PROFILE
A clearheaded and insightful team leader with an ability to bring out the best in the people around me. I have extensive leadership experience in both work and personal life, and thrive on the challenge of creating a happy, cohesive unit.

> Profile offering a quick overview of you as a person, your career objective, your track record, or your key skills. Keep it brief.

EDUCATION AND QUALIFICATIONS

2008 to date
Institute of Chartered Accountants
Masters in Corporate Leadership
Exams this May

> Start with most recent qualifications. Recent graduates should include significant subjects studied and research project and thesis titles if relevant. Also, you don't need to include Leaving results in this case as the Degree and Masters overshadow it.

2005–2008
NUI Maynooth
BA (Honours) Business – 1st class honours
Major Subjects – Business, French

1999–2005
Skerries Community College
Leaving Certificate   Six honours including Irish (C), English (A), Maths (D), French (C), Business Studies (C), Economics (D)

EMPLOYMENT HISTORY

May 2008 to date
Team Leader, Procurement Services
Acme Shoes and Bags

> Start with most recent job, allowing most space to recent and/or relevant positions. Emphasise skills and achievements, using positive language. For example, don't say: "Was responsible for writing policy." Instead say: "Wrote policy on . . ."

- Wrote and delivered procurement policy for entire group
- Negotiated all contracts for 2009 season with international suppliers
- Consistently delivered most fashionable product for highest discount
- Designed new budgeting spreadsheet to streamline purchasing decisions

INTERESTS AND ACHIEVEMENTS

- First class honours degree in Business
- Volunteer on Dublin Simon Community soup runs
- Inter-county volleyball champion

> Avoid the cliché of saying you're interested in hill-walking and reading, unless you actually are. Avoid rehashing your professional achievements and aim to give a broader view of your talents and personality.

REFEREES
Available on request

> Follow this example: don't include actual referees here.

33

Mark O'Reilly
e-mail: mark@gmail.com

Address
5 Northumberland Road,
Ballsbridge,
Dublin 4.
086 1234567

Profile:
A clearheaded and insightful team leader with an ability to bring out the best in the people around me. I have extensive leadership experience in both work and personal life, and thrive on the challenge of creating a happy, cohesive unit.

Education:

2008 to date   **Institute of Chartered Accountants**

Diploma: *Masters in Corporate Leadership*

Results: Pending exams in May

2005–2008   **NUI Maynooth**

Degree: *Bachelor of Arts in Business* – three-year honours degree in Business

Subjects: Business and French

Results: 1:1

1999–2005   **Skerries Community College**
                      Leaving Certificate Results
                      Six honours including Irish (C), English (A), Maths (C), French (B), Business Studies (C), Economics (D)

Employment History: ┌─────────────────────────┐
                                               │ Role outlined clearly   │
                                               └─────────────────────────┘

May 2008 to date   **Team Leader, Procurement Services, Acme Shoes and Bags**

    Manage a team of four procurement staff to source, purchase and deliver best value fashion products for the group.

                      Accomplishments:
                      • Wrote and delivered procurement policy for entire group
                      • Negotiated all contracts for 2009 season with international suppliers
                      • Consistently delivered most fashionable product for highest discount
                      • Designed new budgeting spreadsheet to streamline purchasing decisions.

Additional Activities:
                      • Volunteer on Dublin Simon Community soup runs
                      • Inter-county volleyball champion

34

Skills Profile:

Can work well on my own or as part of a team:
- In my final year in college I worked on a research project team with other people and achieved an overall result of 88%
- Personally researched best practice procurement policies and developed the policy for Group, achieving discount of 15% last year.

Interpersonal and Customer Service Skills:
- Developed an appreciation of the importance of customer service through my work experience.
- Strengthened my communication and interpersonal skills through group projects, class presentations and involvement in the hill-walking club and other societies.

Enthusiastic:
- I am very hard working and enjoy variety and constant challenges.

Where possible, use "and" instead of "&".

Interests & Hobbies:

Keen interest in outdoor activities – hill-walking, cycling and running.
Also enjoy reading and am a member of a local book club.

References available on request

35

MARK O'REILLY

BA (Hons) Business

somename@somehost.ie
Mobile: 086 1234567

PROFILE   A clearheaded and insightful team leader with an ability to bring out the best in the people around me. I have extensive leadership experience in both work and personal life, and thrive on the challenge of creating a happy, cohesive unit.

CAREER HISTORY   **Team Leader, Procurement Services**   May 2008 to date
Acme Shoes and Bags

- Wrote and delivered procurement policy for entire group
- Negotiated all contracts for 2009 season with international suppliers
- Consistently delivered most fashionable product for highest discount
- Designed new budgeting spreadsheet to streamline purchasing decisions

EDUCATION   2008 – to date

Watch the formatting. Make sure margins and indents are all aligned

Masters in Corporate Leadership
Institute of Chartered Accountants

Bachelor of Arts   2005–2008
Business
NUI Maynooth
Major Subjects: Business, French

KEY SKILLS   Strong interpersonal skills gained through extensive study and work experience. Excellent team player, who aims to build strong relationships by respecting the opinions and input of other team members. Motivated self-starter who also takes direction well and is happy to delegate work. Can communicate with ease in difficult situations, e.g. dealing with customer complaints. Organised and computer-literate, with a full working knowledge of the Microsoft Office package as well as the Adobe graphics software and Windows.

INTERESTS   Keen interest in outdoor activities – hill-walking, cycling and running
Volunteer on Dublin Simon Community soup runs
Inter-county volleyball champion

A big block of text such as this looks unattractive and can present a difficulty for the reader to get the important information quickly. Use bullet points instead.

REFERENCES   Available on request

Here is a sample of a good CV for a recent graduate. It still needs a little more work, however.

Paula Murphy

35 High Street, Newtown, Co. Dublin   087 1234567 **punkrocker@yahoo.com**

> This email may have seemed funny when first created, but may seem unprofessional to a prospective employer.

Profile

An enthusiastic and proactive business graduate with a Masters in Marketing. Three years experience working in a marketing role where I have gained valuable experience in developing marketing strategies, including devising communications strategies for leading campaigns. Strong team player, with excellent interpersonal and time management skills. Seeking a challenging role in a dynamic professional environment.

Education and Qualifications

> By justifying to both left and right margins, the text is stretched across the page. Justify left only.

2005–2006   **Smurfit Business School**
             Masters in Marketing
             2.1 Honours

> Increase font size for headings so they stand out. Keep them consistent throughout the CV.

This one-year, full-time masters programme gave me the opportunity to build on the marketing experience I gained at undergraduate level.
Modules included:

- International Marketing
- Strategic Marketing
- Brand Management
- Market Research
- Marketing Communications
- Consumer and Buyer Behaviour

> There is no information about a thesis. An employer will wonder why. Include results here too.

2002-2005   **University College Dublin**
             B Comm.
             2.1 Honours

Final Year Subjects:

- Accounting
- Banking and Finance
- General Management
- International Business
- Marketing
- Management Information System

37

Career History

2006-current   Marketing Matters Inc., Unit 3B Cityside Business Park, Dublin 9

Marketing Matters is a medium-sized business that offers marketing
services to SMEs in a number of industries.

> It should be "men's", not "mens", and "products",
> not "projects". Check your grammar and spelling,
> and get someone else to check your work too.

Key achievements:

- Developed and implemented an integrated marketing strategy for a leading cosmetic
  company to raise awareness of a new mens range of grooming projects prior to
  launch. Product was launched to strong sales, gaining 36% of market share
  within three months.

  > Good evidence
  > of specific
  > results delivered

- Managed the communication campaign and activities, from concept through
  to execution, for the launch of a new line of confectionary products. This
  included devising an advertising campaign, a PR strategy and a successful
  e-marketing campaign.
- Developed new and innovative content for company website including an ePortal with
  interactive user interface.
- Project-managed the launch of an online marketing campaign for new mobile phone
  model. Campaign nominated for "Online Marketing Campaign" award, 2007.

I gained excellent project management and communication skills in this role. It has given me
a thorough understanding of the integrated marketing process.

> Good summary of skills gained
> through the role. Paula could
> have expanded here to say how
> these will apply in the role.

2004–2006   ABC Promotions, 26–28 The Avenue, Dublin 15

ABC Promotions conducts in-store promotional activity for the telecommunications, banking
and leisure industries. I worked as a Promotions Assistant on an ad hoc basis throughout
college.

Duties Included:

- Participated in promotions for key corporate accounts including Mobilefone, Super
  Sports, and Celtic Bank mortgage campaign
- Led a promotional team of ten people whose work involved merchandising and
  conducting promotions for Celtic Bank's new mortgage campaign
- Co-ordinated 15 participants to conduct on-street activity for a Mobilefone product
  awareness campaign.

This role sparked my great interest in Marketing, Promotions and Sales as I enjoyed and
excelled at liaising with brand managers, organising the promotional teams and endorsing the
brands.

> Capital letters not needed
> here. Only use capitals for
> names, titles, places,
> departments etc.

> Justify to the left margin only.

References

Available on Request

38

This sample CV also needs work. Brevity is a good quality, but it is a little too light on important details.

Paula Murphy

35 High Street, Newtown, Co. Dublin

Tel. 087-1234567
Email: PMurphy1987@yahoo.com
Age: 22
Marital status: Single

Age and marital status are not necessary on a CV. Also, an email address such as this probably contains the candidate's year of birth, so should not be used.

Education and Qualifications

2005–2006	Smurfit Business School Masters in Marketing 2.1 Honours
2002–2005	University College Dublin B Comm. 2.1 Honours

Career History

2006–current   Marketing Matters Inc.
Marketing Assistant
Duties include:

No real information about the role or company. Not sure where the jobs were, and few achievements outlined.

- Develop and implement marketing strategy.
- Manage communication campaigns and activities (advertising, PR, e-marketing, liaising with media), from concept through to execution.
- Develop new and innovative content for the website and proactively update existing areas of the website.
- Ownership, management and delivery of projects to high specification, within budget and timeline.
- Other duties as assigned.

2004–2006   ABC Promotions
Promotions Assistant
Duties included:

Beware of American spellings. Set your spellchecker to English (Ireland) or English (UK).

- Celtic Bank mortgage campaign. Worked on promotions for key corporate accounts
- Lead promotional teams whose work involved merchandizing, in-store promotions, on-street activity and special events
- This has sparked my great interest in Marketing, Promotions and Sales as I enjoyed and excelled at liaising with brand managers, organizing the promotional teams and endorsing the brands

Should read "Led"

Interests

Socialising, Restaurants, Cinema, Walking

References

Fr. Michael O'Beirne Principal St. Martin's College Newtown Co. Dublin Tel. 01-1234567	Dr. Maeve Bloggs Lecturer Dept. of Commerce UCD Dublin 4 Tel. 01-1234567

No need to include names and addresses. You can provide these at a later stage. Also, deleting names and addresses will mean this CV can be kept on one page; having so little on one page doesn't look good.

This is a good mid-management CV with a more detailed professional skills profile. There is a gap in the employment dates, however, which any recruiter would question. Five years (1998–2003) is a big gap and she needs to account for that time

Helen Jones

181 Strand Street
Ardmore
Co. Westmeath

This font is Trebuchet MS. While it is a sans-serif font, it is easy enough to read.

Tel: 01 123 4567
Mobile: 087-1234567
Email: firstlastname@gmail.com

PROFESSIONAL PROFILE

Strong professional with a wealth of experience in the financial services sector, predominantly in customer service development; change management; strategic planning and leadership. Key achievements and skills include:

Strategic Vision and Planning

- I am a proven strategic thinker and planner, with the vision and foresight to develop and execute long-term strategies that deliver an organisation's objectives.
- Successfully led a change management programme to implement an automated procurement system that impacted on 1,000 end-users and increased efficiency by x%
- As Customer Services Manager, I led the development of a customer service team to manage all procurement queries from internal and external customers.

Service Development and Management

- I have a proven track record in proactively managing customer services and creating new initiatives to enhance service delivery.
- In my current role, I undertook the recruitment and training of 40 customer service agents, which led to enhanced Service Level Agreements with suppliers.

Leadership and People Management

- Strong people manager and have demonstrated the ability to challenge, lead and motivate a large team to deliver and exceed objectives.

Use simple, direct and action language. Instead of saying "I undertook the recruitment and training of 40 customer service agents", say "I recruited and trained 40 customer . . .".

EMPLOYMENT HISTORY

CURRENT ROLE

Full stop missing

This achievement needs strong editing. It is not clear how well the team is performing today. Specific results and measures of success need to be included.

ABC Bank Inc   **Sept 2003 - Present**

Position: Customer Service Manager

Recruited to establish a Customer Service Department to manage internal and external customer queries relating to payment of invoices, purchase orders, and a newly introduced procurement process

Key objective was to change the culture and instill confidence in our customers. Procurement best practice has been successfully implemented into the day-to-day work of all staff.

Key Achievements:

- Established the Procurement Customer Service Team. The Service is fully established with a 7-person team providing services related to payment of invoices; making purchase requisitions and purchase orders; a centralised procurement process; queries relating to use of an integrated purchasing software and vendor management.

- Created and implemented strong systems for dealing with procurement queries.

- Provided professional advice to Senior Executives, Business Unit managers, vendors and staff in relation to procurement issues.

- Advised Business Unit managers in relation to corporate governance and achieved improvements of ABC.

Watch for repetitive phrases

Watch for inconsistent use of capitals

PROFESSIONAL EDUCATION/TRAINING AND DEVELOPMENT

Trinity College, Dublin.   **2003-2005**
Executive MBA in Financial Services
Modules included Business Ethics and Corporate Responsibility, Performance Driven Marketing, Cross Cultural Management, Strategic Implementation and Management of Change, Project Management and Risk Management.

Dundee University, Scotland   **1998**
Bachelor of Commerce (2.1 honours)

PROFESSIONAL INTERESTS

- Member of National Purchasing Institute
- Member of Chartered Institute of Purchasing and Supply

REFEREES

Available on Request

42

The Executive CV

If you have had a long and varied career, you will need an executive summary at the beginning of your CV, like the previous CV. Spare the recruiter the job of wading through a list of jobs stretching back twenty years across a range of sectors to find the skills relevant to their particular role. Instead, use a comprehensive personal profile at the start of the CV, which describes you, your professional background, and the various roles you have held and in which sectors. You might also include a line explaining your career objectives.

For senior manager and executive roles, recruiters are looking for leadership strengths and skills with a proven track record of delivery. They are particularly interested in those skills that show you can move easily from one industry to another. This is why you should summarise your four or five critical skills in a Key Skills and Achievements section on page one, rather than waiting to outline these skills under each job role.

Under each heading, give two or three examples of achievements that illustrate your strengths in areas such as Strategy and Planning; Leadership and People Management; Managing Stakeholder Relationships; and Delivering Results. For example:

Leadership
- Under my leadership, Company XYZ has expanded from five to thirty stores nationally, and network turnover grew to in excess of €X million.

Delivering Results
- I have successfully led an international cross-functional project team in ABC company that delivered the prime objectives of reducing inventory by €X million and the product range by 50%.

You may also include a heading to highlight your relevant specialisation or technical skills such as marketing or project management as appropriate.

Europass CV

Some organisations request that you use the Europass template to create your CV when applying for positions that they have advertised. The Europass CV is a relatively new initiative that will help you make your skills and qualifications more clearly understood in other European Union countries. It is intended to standardise the look of CVs across the EU so you won't be at a disadvantage because of the style of CV common in your native country.

The Europass CV often contains information such as age, which is not usually suitable in an Irish context, but if they have requested the Europass CV, you should provide all the information specified. You can build your own Europass CV with the help of the website **www.europass.ie**.

Key Components of a Cover Letter

The purpose of a cover letter is to introduce you to the recruiter. It also offers you a chance to stand out from other candidates and increase your chances of being chosen for interview.

A good cover letter has a clear structure:

- ✔ Opening paragraph: should outline why you are interested in the position, and refer to where you identified the job: "I enclose my CV in response to your advertisement in . . ."

- ✔ Middle paragraphs: should outline your current situation and highlight your suitability for the position you are applying for – your "match" for the skills they are looking for.

- ✔ Closing paragraph: should end courteously and state clearly your interest in meeting to discuss the position, e.g. "I am available for interview at your convenience." Type or print your name underneath your signature.

No matter how tempted you are to do so, never send out multiple copies of the same cover letter. Take the time to individualise the letter so that the potential employer reads something that is specific to the job they have advertised and their organisation. We have had countless letters over the years telling us why candidates would love to work for our company – and then naming another organisation.

Pointers for success:

- ✔ Keep your letter to one typed sheet of A4 paper if possible.

- ✔ Address the letter to a particular person by name. Phone to find this out if necessary, e.g. "Dear Mr O'Brien".

- ✔ Use "Yours sincerely" if you know the person's name, and "Yours faithfully" if you were unable to get their name.

- ✔ You may include a heading such as: **Re: Position of Sales Consultant**.

- ✔ Communicate something personal that will grab their attention, e.g. "My industry experience and specialist skills will contribute to your company . . ."

- ✔ Ask yourself "Why should this person want to meet me?" and answer it throughout your letter.

- ✔ As I said earlier, make sure you set "language" to Irish or UK spelling so that you don't use American spellings, e.g. "organization"/"organisation".

- ✔ Look for feedback on what you have written. Show draft forms, letters or CVs to a friend or trusted colleague and seek their opinion.

Sample Cover Letter

Your address
Address
Tel. number
Email address

Date

Recipient's name
Their position
Their company

Their address

Dear Mr O'Malley

I wish to apply for the position of Branch Manager for the Mullingar branch, as advertised in *The Irish Times* last Monday.

I am a key member of the Edenderry branch, with 5 years' experience in the insurance industry. I have a proven track record in delivering results, as demonstrated by the success of my current branch and section.

I am confident that my skills, experience and motivation make me the ideal person to take on this role. My knowledge of the branch and extensive insurance experience will ensure achievement of overall branch objectives.

My key skills include:

- Developing and maintaining business relationships with clients and colleagues
- Organising and planning to ensure achievement of personal targets
- Coaching, managing and monitoring the performance of new and temporary staff to deliver exceptional service
- Recently passed Certificate of Insurance practice exam.

I have demonstrated my ability and readiness to take on this position by deputising for the branch manager on many occasions.

I would bring considerable energy and enthusiasm to the role with the long-term aim of maximising XYZ's business in the midlands.

I would be delighted to discuss my CV with you and outline how I will add value to the Mullingar branch, as Branch Manager.

Yours sincerely

....   Type your name underneath your signature

Application Form Preparation

Some organisations ask you to apply by application form only. A form requires the same level of care as your CV.

Some pointers:

- Type it, don't handwrite it. The forms are usually available online, and are much easier to read if typed. Remember that the interview board will be reading lots of applications. They do not want to struggle to decipher poor handwriting.

- Most application forms will cover the same material that you have on your CV, but some may ask more specific questions on the following areas:

  ✔ **Competency-based questions**: These questions look for evidence of your approach and competence in a given situation; e.g. *"Give an example of a time when you worked in a team"* or *"Describe your role, and outline the end result"*. See page 68 for more detail on preparing competency examples.

  ✔ **Motivational questions**: These questions are designed to identify what motivates you; to find out why are you applying, what your career goals are, what appeals to you about the job, field or industry. You may be asked: *"Outline why you are interested in this job, and what personal qualities and skills you have that make you suitable?"*

- When deciding on the examples to use in your application form, pick ones that show the required competency most clearly. Write them out factually and clearly.

- Sometimes the same example may illustrate two different competencies – but try to use different examples.

- Ensure that you take credit for your achievements. Use phrases such as "I was responsible for . . ." Application forms and interviews are not places for false modesty. If you were the person responsible, then say so. Equally, if you shared the responsibility, say so.

- When you have finished filling out the form, leave it for a few hours, or until the next day. Then come back and look at it with fresh eyes.

- Check your spellings. Remember that a spellcheck will not pick up some mistakes: its/it's, too/to, from/form, practice/practise, there/their, you're/your. Ideally, get somebody else to proofread your work.

- You will need to remember exactly what you wrote, so photocopy or save a copy of your completed form. Before you send it, print a copy and keep it on your file for future reference.

Chapter 4

Marketing Yourself

Effective marketing brings the benefits of a product to the relevant audiences. You can speed up your career change and get a job you are more suited to by applying a proactive marketing approach to the process.

You need to be clear on your product: YOU, your unique experience and skills. You need to understand your audiences or potential employers, and what exactly they are looking for in the ideal candidate. And finally, you must be really clear on how you will help them and contribute to the company.

In this chapter I will take you through the steps to effectively market yourself and conduct an effective job search.

This chapter is divided into the following sections:

- Planning to Market Yourself
- Starting your Job Search
    - Advertisements
    - Recruitment Agencies, Consultants, and Executive Search Firms
    - Networking
    - Speculative Approaches
- Organising Your Job Search

Planning to Market Yourself

Marketing yourself to prospective employers means matching your skills and CV to the requirements of the roles they have on offer. However, many jobs are not advertised. Agencies could have a range of roles that might suit your skills. So, you'll need to vary your approach with each.

Key Steps

1. Using the forms in Chapter 1 and 2 of the book, identify your main areas of interest and where potential job opportunities might lie. Don't limit

49

your search just to jobs that are similar to your most recent one. Consider a broad range of:

- Market sectors
- Industries
- Positions and roles

2. Identify where to look for jobs:
    - Advertisements
    - Recruitment agencies, consultancies and executive search firms
    - Networking
    - Speculative approaches

3. Plan how you will approach each of these.

Starting your Job Search

Advertisements

1. Make a list of places where you will find advertisements for the type of roles you are looking for. You should include publications, websites, job centres and other sources e.g.
    - *Evening Herald/Evening Echo*
    - *Sunday Independent* Business section
    - *The Irish Times* Business section
    - *Belfast Telegraph*
    - *Irish Examiner*
    - www.nixers.com
    - www.jobs.ie
    - www.publicjobs.ie
    - Regional newspapers
    - Professional and specialist publications

2. Review the range of roles. Don't limit yourself just to familiar occupations at this stage. Focus on the skills and requirements of the roles that interest you.

3. Assess how your skills, strengths and experience match what is advertised.

4. Research the organisation and role.

5. Tailor your CV and write a cover letter that sells your suitability for the role.

6. Follow up with a call (if necessary) to check progress on your application.

7. If an advertisement is being handled by an agency or recruitment consultancy firm, it is often worth ringing them first to discuss the role before you apply. Then follow steps 3–6. You may also want to register with them for other possible positions.

Treat all communication with agencies as if they were part of a formal interview process. You will need to sell yourself effectively to the agency to ensure they can sell you to an employer.

Recruitment Agencies, Consultants and Executive Search firms

Many organisations use recruitment agencies to handle the initial screening of applicants. Register with several suitable job agencies to begin with. Select agencies that specialise in your field of work or that come recommended to you from someone you trust. Select those that have a good reputation – they may have won awards or sponsor awards.

The key to success with agencies is to develop a relationship with the consultant who will be working with and for you. You need to be sure they are putting you forward for the most suitable roles and that they are selling your skills.

1. Draw up a list of agencies you might approach and register with.

2. Include those that specialise in the industry or roles you are interested in.

3. Call them and talk to the person specialising in your area. Outline your career objectives and the areas and roles you are interested in. Outline your core skills and experience. Send them your CV.

4. Arrange to meet the consultant who will now be marketing you to prospective employers. Prepare for this meeting as if you are going for a real interview.

5. You need to sell yourself to them before they will sell you to potential employers. Remember to sell your knowledge, skills and experience and link it to the role.

6. Ask them lots of questions about the role and the organisation. Find out where the role fits in the organisation. What will you be doing on a daily basis? What will your objectives and deliverables be like? You should ask plenty of questions about the role to be sure you are fully informed. For instance, knowing that the role is mainly commission-driven or involves a lot of cold-calling may change your mind about applying.

7. Make notes of the meeting and the next steps that were agreed.

8. Follow up with an email to say thanks.

9. Don't limit yourself to one agency. But don't stretch yourself either by applying to every one. Be selective.

10. Keep in regular contact with them to ensure you get placed – but don't pester them.

List the main agencies you might contact:

- *Career Start Consulting - 014987654*
- *Procurementjobs.ie*
- *etc. . . .*

Make sure your recruitment consultant lets you know about every job they have you in mind for. Your CV should be tailored for each role. You should write a fresh cover letter for each application, showing how your skills match the requirements of the job. Remember, the cover letter is where you outline the benefits to the employer; how you will help them and contribute in the role. Ask the agency to send this with your application.

The following example from Yvonne, a client of mine, shows that a considered approach beats a rushed one and that a poor job agency could do more harm than good.

After my lay-off, I sent my CV to lots of relevant agencies in Ireland and Britain, but I had had no success and started to investigate why.

I had only sent CVs, not cover letters, and some of the agencies simply forwarded my CV to prospective employers. So no cover letters went out; no personal note to help me stand out from other applicants.

Because so many agencies had received my CV, it was only a matter of time before one of my target employers received my CV from two different agencies. And to make matters worse, one agency had an older version of my CV, so two different versions of my CV had arrived at this employer's office.

Always tell your agency to contact you before they issue your CV to any prospective employer. Always prepare a short note or cover letter for each application.

Networking

Many candidates underestimate how important and valuable their network can be to their future career. Today the big issue is getting your CV onto the desk of the HR manager or the hiring manager. Furthermore, an employer is more likely to trust someone who comes recommended by an existing employee. Networking alone won't get you the job but it can help to get you to an interview. After that, it's up to you! Let key people in your social and professional circle know that you're looking for a new job.

Frank's experience demonstrates the power of having a strong network.

I was applying for a senior position (Chief Financial Officer) and submitted a CV and good cover letter to the relevant executive search company. They were very nice, but explained that my application was one of many and that I shouldn't get my hopes up.

I had made a point of staying in touch with several of my former college friends who had progressed over the years to senior positions in the same industry that I was hoping to enter. Over lunch with one friend, I told him that I was hoping to fill the vacancy in Company X, but didn't seem to have much hope. He said that he knew the HR director in the actual company (not the executive search company) and that he would forward my CV to her directly.

The outcome was that the HR director looked at my CV, and then forwarded it to the executive search company telling them that she wanted me to be interviewed. I know the interview came about because of my networking only.

And yes, I got the job. Not only that, but now I'm particularly receptive to jobseekers who hope to network through me.

To make the most of your network of contacts, start by identifying the people you know who can point you in the direction of a job or assist you in your job search. Make a list of people in each area and prioritise them. Use the following table:

My Network Contact List

Personal Contacts	Friends of Contacts
•	•
•	•
•	•
•	•
•	•
•	•
Industry/Business Contacts	Friends of Contacts
•	•
•	•
•	•
•	•
•	•
•	•
Other Contacts, e.g. clubs, schools	Friends of Contacts
•	•
•	•
•	•
•	•
•	•
•	•

Making the Contact

1. Decide whether to call or write initially.
2. Introduce yourself and say who gave you their name.
3. Ask for advice, direction or help with your job search.
4. Arrange a suitable time to call or meet up.
5. Explain what you're looking for and briefly outline your background and skills.
6. Listen very carefully as these leads can provide you with valuable
   - referrals
   - industry information and knowledge
   - and most importantly, possible job opportunities.
7. Give them your contact details.
8. Send a short thank you note or email. Enclose your CV if they ask for it. Keep in touch with them.

Set up a spreadsheet or table like the one below and list the key people you will contact first.

My Network

Name	Company	Role	Date contacted	Action taken	Next steps/ Progress

Speculative Approaches

A speculative approach is one in which you target organisations you are interested in working with, even when no vacancy has been advertised. The key steps of a speculative approach include:

1. Identify and prioritise your target organisations.
2. Research the organisation so you can tailor your approach.
3. Go back to your network and see if you have contacts who could help with your research. If you do, follow the steps above.

55

4. Send your CV to the correct person with a cover letter outlining:
   - Your request for a meeting to discuss possibilities
   - Your skills, experience and achievements
   - The role and types of opportunities you are seeking
   - How you believe you could add value to their organisation

5. Follow up with a phone call.

Organising Your Job Search

Conducting an effective job search requires discipline, good organisational skills and rigorous time management. This means:

- ✔ Creating a system for managing all the paperwork and appointments that your job search will generate.

- ✔ Careful planning and prioritising of your activities so you achieve your objectives.

Organising a System

As you begin your job search, your tasks and activities will multiply, so the earlier you get organised the better. You will need easy access to all your relevant documentation and contacts, so that your plan and follow-up is effectively managed. It is easy to miss important information or details if you don't keep track of information. Set up folders and Excel files to record critical information such as:

- ✔ Agency contacts

- ✔ Jobs applied for and responses

- ✔ Interview details

- ✔ Research and details of companies

- ✔ Speculative approaches made

- ✔ Names and addresses of all network contacts

Organising Your Time

✔ Have a plan

✔ Get a diary and schedule tasks and deadlines

✔ Allocate times for each activity and task in your job search, e.g. contact agencies, meet agencies, amend CV.

✔ Try to establish a daily routine, e.g.
- 9:00–10:00   Internet search
- 10:00–10:30   Read papers
- 10:30–11:30   Ring agencies
- 14:00–17:00   Meet agencies

Remember, finding a job can be a full-time job in itself. Make good use of your time. Once you have a plan, you are more likely to stick to it.

Other Practical stuff . . .

✔ Get yourself a proper email address

✔ Record a professional voice message for your mobile and home telephones

✔ Set up a personal profile online using professional networking sites such as LinkedIn. Be sure to set up the proper security settings and that the material you include is relevant to the roles you are applying for.

✔ Google yourself, because that's what your employer will do. Based on what you find, tidy up your content on any other personal or social networking sites such as Bebo or Facebook. Also check out other search engines such as Yahoo and Bing.com.

Mary, a client of ours, took a couple of weeks' "time out" to step back before embarking on her job search. A good idea? Yes, if you have the discipline to give it your full energy afterwards.

However, Mary found it very hard to get back into the job/career search mode after her break. Mary came to me and we worked out a daily and weekly plan for her. As she was an experienced administrator, she managed this really well, and after a few days was in a routine that was paying off. She set up folders and files to track correspondence so she could put her hand on all the relevant documentation whenever she got a call. She also scheduled at least two meetings per week with previous colleagues and others from her network.

Chapter 5

Preparing for Interview

Your CV may be very impressive, your cover letter excellent and there may be a variety of other reasons why you are good enough to get the job, but none of this matters if you don't do a good interview. A good CV will get you to an interview, but it won't carry you through it.

To perform well at interview, you will need to prepare properly. This part of the book is designed to take you through the steps to help you become a better interviewee.

Over the next two chapters, we'll highlight the areas you'll need to prepare and the key components of a good interview under the following headings:

- Understanding Interview Types
- Getting Ready for Interview
- Preparing in Detail
  - ○ Step 1 – Plan your Agenda
  - ○ Step 2 – Anticipate key questions
  - ○ Step 3 – Build your Answers and Examples
  - ○ Step 4 – Rehearse and Practise (out loud)
- Communicating Effectively
- Top Tips from Interview Board Members

Understanding Interview Types

There are a number of different types of interviews:

1. The "just come in for a chat" interview
2. The traditional interview
3. The semi-structured interview
4. The structured or competency-based interview
5. The telephone interview

Treat them all with the same level of respect; they are all important. Prepare fully.

1. **The "just come in for a chat" interview**

   This type of interview tends to be quite informal. The interview may happen when you have a personal contact within the organisation or someone on your network passed on your CV.

   This type of interview mostly happens in the private sector, and only rarely in the public service. Prepare for the meeting as if it were a real interview.

2. **The traditional interview**

   Most interviews are conducted in the traditional manner. Broadly speaking the interview board will go through your CV and probe each role to see if you have the skills required for the position. They will look for evidence of your achievements and strengths and possibly your weaknesses. They may also ask for specific ideas or suggestions you have about the role.

   Your degree of success in the interview will depend on several factors:

   ✔ Your skill as an interviewee

   ✔ Your communication skills

   ✔ The types of questions you are asked

   ✔ Your knowledge of the company and job

   ✔ How you handle unexpected questions.

3. **The semi-structured interview**

   Semi-structured interviews can best be described as a hybrid of the traditional interview and a competency-based interview. In this type of interview, the interviewers decide on several clear criteria or competencies by which they will judge your suitability. They will ask you questions based around the criteria but they could also ask you questions on related (or unrelated) topics. You may or may not be aware of these criteria in advance. But you can be sure they will focus on the job, your CV and experience and any technical or specialist competencies required for the role, as well as other skills such as communication, people and interpersonal skills, and organising and planning skills.

Semi-structured interviews have become more common in recent years. They offer more flexibility than the structured competency-based interviews and have the advantage of allowing for a greater exchange of ideas between you and the interview panel.

4. The structured or competency-based interview

The competency-based interview generally identifies around five or six competencies considered necessary for the job in question. Public service interviews and application forms are competency-based. Many organisations in the private sector also use this method for selecting candidates, especially multinationals, banks and some semi-state organisations.

The specific competencies are usually clearly identified and explained in the job application material. During the interview, you will be expected to give examples to demonstrate that you have these competencies. These examples should mostly be based on your work experience.

The interviewers will ask you questions based on your examples. Their questions are designed to be probing and to find out what exactly you did, how you did it, what obstacles you overcame and what the outcome was. The interviewers will also want to know if you learned from the experience.

You may be asked to give an example other than those you gave on your application form, for any competency. So it is important that you prepare a second example – just in case.

The advantages of the competency-based interview process:

✔ You know exactly what topics will be discussed.

✔ You have a chance to prepare your best examples.

✔ You will be asked about the same competencies as every other candidate.

✔ There is a clear marking system that ensures greater fairness, objectivity and consistency.

✔ There should be no questions asked on unrelated topics.

5. The telephone interview

Increasingly, employers are using telephone interviews at the earlier stages of the screening process. If you are applying for jobs abroad, often your first contact with the employer will be over the phone. And while it may seem to lack the formality of a more traditional "face-to-face" panel interview, you must prepare for the phone interview just as you would prepare for a meeting in person.

Make sure that you are free to make or take the call at the pre-arranged time. Not being free to talk at this time is akin to missing or turning up late for an interview. However, if an employer calls you out of the blue at an inconvenient time, politely ask if you could call back at a more convenient time. Set yourself up in a quiet room where you know you won't be disturbed. Where possible, use a landline number. We all know how susceptible mobile calls are to "breaking up" and a "Hello? Hello?" situation needs to be avoided at all costs.

Be aware that all non-verbal communication will be absent in a phone interview. Posture, body language and eye contact will be missing from the equation. So your tone of voice will need to be confident and enthusiastic. If necessary, rehearse and record yourself beforehand to make sure your enthusiasm is coming across in your voice. Similarly, you will find it difficult to gauge the reaction of the panel when you cannot see them. Silences in an interview can be tricky at the best of times and this can be even more pronounced in a phone interview. If you need time to think of an answer, tell the panel you are taking a moment to think so they know you are still on the other end of the line.

The main advantage of a telephone interview is that you can have your notes close by and can refer to them during the interview. So have your CV or application form to hand. You should work out the requirements of the role and jot down examples of where you have demonstrated these skills in the past. Be sure to arrange these pages in an orderly manner so that you do not have to rummage through sheets of paper in order to find examples. Recently a client of ours completed a phone interview with his sitting room wall covered in flip chart pages full of notes and examples. Also, you can take some notes as the interview progresses so you can keep track of the questions being asked.

If you suspect you will be getting phone calls from employers to either arrange a phone interview or to conduct an impromptu interview, make sure you record a personal, professional message on your voicemail so that employers can leave you a message if you are unavailable to take the call.

Getting Ready for Interview

Most people find interviews a nerve-wracking experience, but with the correct preparation, you can control – and even enjoy – the process. Preparing your CV or application form was already a significant step in preparing for your interview.

If you've followed my earlier advice of tailoring each application you should have completed the initial preparation steps of:

1. **Researching** the job role and the company.

2. **Reflecting on** your own skills, knowledge, abilities and experience and knowing which are most relevant for the job.

3. **Revising** your CV or application form - so it contained your most relevant skills and competencies.

It is important that you now give yourself adequate time to prepare for the interview. No matter how impressive your experience and how well it is represented on your CV, your interview alone will determine if you get the job.

The successful candidate will be the one who proves to the interview board that they clearly understand the role and what's going to be involved, and that they have what it takes to do the job well.

Many candidates believe that their CV and track record will speak for itself, particularly if they are going for internal roles where their track record is known. Not so. You will only be scored on what you **say** in the forty-five minutes in the interview room.

At the interview, you should always assume you're starting with a blank slate. You need to be able to present your track record and achievements to the interviewers so that they are in *no doubt* about your capability for the job in question. And remember, the interviewers are judges, not advocates. So don't expect someone you know on the interview board to make the case for you after the interview when the board are discussing your performance.

Whether or not your interview is classified as a competency-based interview, you should prepare as if it is. You need to work out which achievements, projects and work experience you intend to talk about to demonstrate your ability in different areas. Look back over the last few years; there will be recent projects or tasks from your Achievement Matrix which you can use to show your ability to make decisions, to work with people, and to organise and manage for results. Select your best examples to demonstrate that you have the required competencies and experience.

Go back over the key areas you prepared and researched before, and reflect on:

✔ the job role and where it fits in the company

✔ the competencies and skills required

✔ your own strengths and achievements and suitability for the role.

Preparing in Detail

The best way to prepare for the interview is to follow these four simple steps:

- Step 1 – Plan your Agenda
- Step 2 – Anticipate key questions
- Step 3 – Build your answers and examples
- Step 4 – Rehearse and practise (out loud)

Step 1 – Plan your Agenda

You should be going into the interview with a clear agenda. You should know the items you want to communicate to the interviewers, even if you're not asked for them.

Make a list of all the things the interviewers must know about you when the interview is over. These will fall roughly into three areas:

1. Your understanding of the **job role** and the **"step-up"** or **transition** involved.

2. Your **career history** including relevant experience, key achievements and why you match what is required.

63

3. Your **specific examples** of how and when you have demonstrated the skills and competencies required, plus back-up examples.

Other areas you could include on your agenda are:

- ✔ Your **key priorities** in the job if you were successful, your business plan and vision

- ✔ Your knowledge of current **industry or business challenges** or issues relating to the role

- ✔ Any **recommendations**, suggested changes or opportunities you see for developing the role

- ✔ Areas requiring **development** for both yourself and the organisation.

Step 2 – Anticipate key questions

We cannot predict the exact questions you'll be asked in the interview. However, we can anticipate the main areas of questioning that interviewers are likely to focus on. You need to anticipate the likely questions within these areas and prepare for these so that the interviewers are clear about how your skills and experience are a fit for the role.

Think of the interview process as a funnel, where the interviewer is gathering the general details of your experience at the top in order to gain a broad understanding of your capability. As the funnel narrows down, the interviewer will gather more specific examples of your experience and technical competence to match against the job requirements. Finally, at the bottom of the funnel the interviewer will ask clarifying questions so they have the critical information to be confident in your ability to do the job.

At the start of the interview the interviewer will tend to ask broad, **open questions** about your experience and track record. Their aim is to help you relax and to get you to open up and talk. Typically, their questions will include:

- ✔ Give me a concise overview of your career to date

- ✔ What are the main highlights of your CV?

- ✔ Why do you think you are suitable for the role?

After you have had a chance to describe what happened, the interviewer will follow up with **probing questions** to clarify details. These are the "who", "what", "when", "where", "why" and "how" questions, and will be used to elicit details about your role, your personal approach, the behaviours you used and the outcomes. In doing so the interviewer is trying to ascertain exactly what you did, why you did it and what happened as a result. Examples of probing questions include:

- ✔ What was your particular role on the team?
- ✔ How many were on the team?
- ✔ How did you contribute to the team?
- ✔ What exactly did you do on a typical day?
- ✔ What effect did that have on your team morale?
- ✔ How did you feel about what happened?
- ✔ What was the result?
- ✔ Did it work?
- ✔ What happened when you introduced those new procedures or cutbacks?
- ✔ How did you measure the success?
- ✔ Why did you do it that way?
- ✔ Would you do it the same way again? If not, why?

Insight from an experienced interviewer:

> My favourite questions are "Why?", "How come?", and "What then?". I like to keep the interviewee talking. I listen to hear how they coped in particular circumstances, and to hear what they learned from their experiences. Usually I present them with a realistic crisis, and ask what they would do in that circumstance. Then I sit back and ask "Why?" to almost all their answers. It unnerves them sometimes, but it lets me see how they cope under pressure and really see how they handled a situation.

Here are the main areas of questioning you need to focus on and be prepared for. In many cases, a typical interview will follow a very similar structure and sequence.

1. **CV-based questions**
   - Tell me about yourself.
   - Can you take us through your CV?
   - Tell me about your current role.

2. **Questions about the job role**
   - Why are you applying for this job?
   - What are the key challenges for you in this role?
   - What will your priorities be in this role?

3. **Skills and competency-based questions**
   - Tell me about a time when you managed change?
   - Are you a good project manager/communicator/organiser?
   - Tell me about your analytical skills.

4. **Strengths and Weaknesses questions**

5. **Where do you see yourself in five years' time?**

6. **Why You?**

7. **Nasty or tough questions**

8. **Any questions? Anything you'd like to add?**

1. **CV-based questions**

The opening questions at interviews are designed to relax you and get you talking. This is also where the interviewer is looking for the highlights of your experience at the beginning in order to gain a broad understanding of your capability. Questions like *"Give us an overview of your career to date"* or *"Take us through your CV"* can set the tone for the rest of the interview – positively or negatively.

Use your CV to structure your answer. This initial introductory piece must be well prepared. This is your chance to get the interview off to a good start. Introduce yourself well and present a clear summary of your career and education. Be ready to answer questions about why you moved and made the choices you made.

Take the interviewers through the highlights of your career. Be brief and concise. Remember, this should be a "whistle-stop tour" through your CV and not a "walk down memory lane". This is key as, all too often in my experience, when asked for a brief overview, candidates launch into a ten minute monologue, hardly pausing for breath. All this achieves is to confirm to the interviewer that they didn't listen to the original question, and their ability to communicate clearly and concisely is questionable.

As you talk through your career emphasise the most relevant jobs, stating your role and, in a few lines, explain what you did. Highlight your contribution and main achievements. Emphasise specific skills you developed, particularly those that are transferable to the new job. Be prepared for questions about any gaps in employment or short periods in companies.

This is your opportunity to lead the interview and outline your agenda. So have this well prepared. Rehearse. Be positive, enthusiastic and interesting.

2. Questions about the job role

Be ready at any stage of the interview for specific questions relating to the role. You should be proving your suitability for the role by outlining:

✔ your understanding of the role and your priorities if successful

✔ the key responsibilities you will have in the role

✔ how you will deliver on these.

You need to show clearly why you want to work for the company and your motivation for the job. Show how you see yourself in the role in the organisation. Know how you will add value and contribute in the job.

Also be prepared for questions about how you will manage the **transition** into the role, particularly if you are changing sectors. If the new role is a promotion for you, you will also need to show how you will manage the **"step-up"** and increase in responsibility and accountability.

When preparing your answers, make sure you link your experience to the priorities in the job role. Bring in relevant information and details you know about the role and organisation.

Don't make the mistake of listing off facts you read in the organisation's annual report or website without showing how they relate to the job. Whilst this shows you did some homework it doesn't really impress. What the interviewer wants to see and hear is that you are genuinely interested in the company and the role; that you have thought carefully about why you are applying for the position and understand what is required.

Sometimes interviewers will ask **scenario**-type questions about the job, where they outline a typical scenario you could encounter if you were successful, and they'll ask you how would manage it. You could give the interviewers a run-through as to how you would handle the situation – however, depending on how you present this, it could sound like a text-book answer. On the other hand, if you use an example to illustrate how you handled a similar situation in the past, and relate this to the role, now you are providing more concrete evidence of your skills and showing how you'll use them. Use the answer structure on page 73 to help you prepare relevant examples you might use in the interview.

3. Skills and competency-based questions

In most interviews, and in particular those based on a clear set of competencies, you should provide specific examples that demonstrate your ability and experience in each of the skill and competency areas required. You need to show the depth and breadth of your experience.

Interviewers will often ask for a **specific example** of a time where you demonstrated or used a particular skill or competency. For instance:

- Tell me about a time when you had to deal with a staff member who was not pulling their weight.

- Can you give me an example of a time you had to manage a dispute between two colleagues?

Try to use different examples for the different skills and competencies, even though one example may actually cover two or three skills. You don't want to be seen as a "one-trick pony".

Think back over your previous work experience and start gathering evidence you can use at your interview. First, list all the critical skills and competencies required for the role. You may find this has already been provided for you as part of the recruitment process. Next, think through your previous work experience and list key projects, deliverables, activities and achievements that effectively highlight your ability in each of the areas – refer to your Life and Career Path Template on page 3 and My Key Achievements Matrix on page 5.

A useful way of compiling this information is to draw up a simple form to capture your relevant examples for each skill. The form may look something like this:

Critical skills/ competencies for role	Examples from Current role	Examples from Previous role	Previous role . . . and so on
Team player	*Project A – achieved X* *Project B– delivered Y*	*Project C – delivered Z* *Project D – delivered V*	*Project E – result W*
Communication	*Project A* *Project H*	*Project I–achieved U*	*Project Z*
People management	*and so on . . .*		
Project management			

The next step will be to get these examples and evidence of your ability on paper, clearly and concisely. See Step 3 on page 72.

4. Strengths and Weaknesses questions

What are your strengths?

You may be asked questions about your strengths and weaknesses. Go back to the Transferable Skills Audit you completed in Chapter 1 and the model above and identify your skills that will be most relevant. Be prepared to summarise your top three or four strengths that will be key to your success in the role. Highlight some of your achievements and be prepared to explain them, showing how you applied the skills and the results you delivered. Outline how your strengths equip you for the role.

Do you have any weaknesses?

This question can cause difficulty for a lot of people. Your answer to this question is not about "shooting yourself in the foot", but should demonstrate that you have a genuine sense of self-awareness of your own shortcomings and are prepared to address them. Review the development areas you identified earlier in the Skills Audit and select a weakness that you can rectify with training or learn to improve e.g. a skill. Don't select a personality trait as a weakness, because these are much harder to change.

Otherwise, give an example of a weakness you have recently addressed, and state the steps and measures you took to overcome it. Be genuine. Be sure to emphasise that this weakness is not going to get in the way of you doing a great job.

Do not say you have no weaknesses. Also avoid the most clichéd responses to this question: "I am a perfectionist" or "I work too hard".

5. Where do you see yourself in five years' time?

A little forethought is required to answer this question effectively. Realistically, where *could* you be in five years' time, taking today and this job as your starting point? Be realistic. If you are CEO material, then say it. If you aren't, you might seem naïve by showing such lofty ambitions.

It is important that you relate your answer to your planned success in the role; i.e. achieving your vision and delivering in the role. You should also show that your ambitions lie within the organisation and that you'd love an opportunity to develop further in the organisation, into area X, Y or Z. If you've plans to study, say so. If you would like to broaden your skills, say so too.

6. Why You?

This is another question that candidates often find tricky, but only because they don't prepare properly for it. This question will be asked in some way, shape or form during the interview. It could be asked in any of the following ways:

- What will you bring to the role?
- How will you add value and contribute to the team?
- What makes you different?
- Why do you want this job? What is the fit?

You need to provide a comprehensive answer that will cover all of these areas. So my advice is to answer the question that you were asked, first. Then add in the other three parts to support your answer. Have two or three key points to make for each and present them concisely and confidently, clearly showing why you are the best candidate.

Remember, this is your chance to "sell" yourself. Don't be shy or embarrassed to talk positively about yourself; no-one else is there to do it for you. If you speak in a confident, genuine way, it will not be perceived as arrogance but rather self-belief.

7. Nasty or tough questions

If there are any questions you don't want to be asked, or questions that you found uncomfortable in the past, prepare for them. Rehearse them. Test them with someone whose advice you trust.

Occasionally an interviewer will throw a bit of a curved ball question at you, like, *"If you were a brand of car, which car would you be?"* If this happens, take a moment to think about your answer and then respond, picking a make that allows you to work your strengths into the answer.

8. Any questions? Anything you'd like to add?

This is generally the last question you'll be asked at the interview. Be ready for it. It is the interviewers' way of telling you the interview is almost over. If you have genuine questions about the role – ones that you couldn't have found the answer to prior to the interview – ask them. However, avoid asking questions that show you haven't done your research and preparation fully. That said, if the person has said something about the role that you are unsure about, then don't be afraid to ask a clarifying question.

Either way, rather than just saying, "No, I don't have any questions", use the time as an opportunity to present one last pitch summarising why you are the right person for the job. Highlight the personal strengths, skills, competencies and qualities that will enable you to add value in the role. Whatever you do, don't waste this chance to impress the interviewers one last time. For example:

"No, I've no questions to ask, I'm very clear on what's required in the role, as I did a lot of research into the role myself. Before we finish I'd like to reiterate that the main skills required for the job are the same as those that were critical to me achieving my objectives and delivering results in my current role. I am clear on the priorities and challenges in this role, and I'd really look forward to the opportunity to prove myself and lead this department to achieve the sales strategy."

Step 3 - Build your Answers and Examples

The next step in your preparation is to build and structure your answers for the questions you are likely to be asked. Likewise prepare how you will present the key points you want to make from your own agenda. Remember, an interview is not an oral exam; it's an opportunity for you to illustrate that *you* can do the job. You need to build your answers in advance to all the areas outlined already and practise talking them through – out loud.

When responding to an interviewer who is looking for an example of how you have displayed a particular skill or competency, a good answer should have four different parts:

1. Overview of your experience and track record
2. Specific example
3. Learning and insight
4. Relevance to the job

The following table shows a potential answer using this structure in response to a specific competency question like:

"Tell me about a time when you had to lead your team through a period of transition . . ."

or as broad a question as:

"Are you a good team leader?"

	Suggested Structure	Sample Response
Part 1	A brief overview of your track record, experience and knowledge of the skill or competency required	*"Throughout my career I have had to lead a variety of teams through difficult changes and periods of uncertainty."*
Part 2	A specific example that demonstrates your core skills	*"For example, we recently had to restructure our department and a number of people in my team were impacted by the change. It was my role to lead the team through this time and to ensure we continued to deliver our services effectively."*
Part 3	Personal learning or insights What worked well and why? What would you do differently?	*"During the early weeks of the change I realised I wasn't giving people enough opportunities to ask me questions. I quickly realised that communication was going to be the key to ensuring morale remained positive throughout the change. I learnt that my priority was making sure I talked people through what was happening and gave them a chance to ask questions."*
Part 4	Relevance to the job role	*"This role will require the effective leadership of change. I believe my vast experience of working with teams through periods of transition make me a highly suitable candidate . . ."*

Preparing your Examples and Achievements

Take a sheet of paper for each example and write out the details using the structure above. For each achievement or example identified, there are some key questions you need to consider, such as:

- What was the situation/issue/objective/problem?
  - What were you hoping to do/expected to do?
  - What was the outcome achieved?
- What steps did you take to achieve that particular outcome?
  - What exactly did you do and how did you use your strengths?
  - How did you organise the tasks? Why did you choose to do this?
  - Who else was involved?
  - What did you do in particular that helped to progress things?
  - What challenges or obstacles did you face and how did you overcome them?
  - What challenges did you have to overcome in terms of working with other people?
  - To ensure you don't omit any key details, ask yourself who, what, when, where, why and how?
- What was the end result of your actions?
  - How did things turn out?
  - How did you know it went well?
  - How did you measure this?
  - Were there any broader measures of success or knock-on effects as a consequence?
  - Why was this outcome a personal achievement for you?

Think of this as telling a story – keep it factual and use simple language. At all times try to describe what you did in the first person: "*I* did this because *I* thought this would be the outcome", and so on. Often when describing a situation people fall into the trap of saying, "*we* did this and *we* did that". The interviewer wants to hear what you did yourself.

Now review what you have written and make any amendments. Check that the sequence of events is correct. Reflect on the reasons why you did what you did.

Complete this process for all of your examples. Practise talking each of them through fully. By doing this, you should be very comfortable when you talk through each of them on the interview day and you should not be thrown by probing questions the interviewers might ask.

Step 4 – Rehearse and Practise (out loud)

The more you prepare, the more confident you will be on the day. Get comfortable talking through your examples and answers. If you only rehearse the answers in your head, you won't communicate as fluently as you'd like to or are capable of. The more you talk them through out loud, the more you will internalise the details of the situation, and the sequence of events will flow more naturally.

If you know someone who is an experienced interviewer, ask them if they would be willing to help you with a practice run. You need to hear yourself saying your proposed answers out loud, as this will allow you to adapt what you plan to say. If you don't have someone who can help, then rehearse your proposed answers out loud yourself.

Chapter 6

Communicating at the Interview

How you communicate and present yourself on the day will be determined by the amount of preparation you do. If you've worked through the steps in Chapter 5, you should be well prepared for all potential questions. In addition, if you dress well you will boost your self-confidence, and reduce the impact that the nerves and stress associated with interviews can have. There are some simple steps you can take to ensure you are prepared and ready to:

- communicate effectively
- dress for success
- handle any stress.

Let's start with how you communicate at the interview.

Communicating Effectively

You can only be assessed on the basis of your performance at the interview. Therefore, it is vital that you are clear on your own agenda – the things the interviewers must know about you when you leave the room. *You* must find opportunities to bring these into the conversation.

Don't leave the room thinking: "I wanted to talk about my leadership skills, but they never asked me about them."

Remember:

- Your interview is not an oral examination where you answer the question, hope the answer was the correct one and then wait for the next question.

- You are at interview to prove your ability to deliver and fit into the organisation.

- To show you can operate in the role (or at the next level), you must tell the interviewer you can and then provide the evidence – track record and experience – that this is the case.

- Your communication skills and body language need to reflect the self-confidence and influence required at the appropriate level of the role. Be confident enough to pause and think for a minute if you need to.

- You will also need to engage with the interviewers throughout the interview. As you walk into the interview room, how you relate with the interview board will be watched. Smile, make good eye contact. Shake hands with the members of the interview board, unless they specifically say there is no need. Use their names as appropriate. Speak clearly and concisely – if you have been rehearsing out loud, this will pay off.

Don't rely on the fact that a piece of information is on your application form or CV. Your track record or past performance cannot speak for itself on the day. You need to present the interviewers with the evidence they are looking for.

In addition to the preparation you put in for the interview, there are some key points to remember on the day:

- ✔ Be early. Aim to arrive ten to fifteen minutes early; this will give you time to settle down and gather your thoughts.

- ✔ Know exactly where you are going. Do a test run in the days before just to be sure.

- ✔ Turn off your mobile phone.

Top Tips from Experienced Interview Board Members

- ✔ **Prepare, prepare, prepare** – know about the role or position you are applying for, the priorities involved and, most importantly, the skills and qualities required.

- ✔ **Be able to talk about your own experience** – when you used these skills and qualities and how they are relevant for the job role.

✔ **Be friendly and enthusiastic during the interview** – the interviewers want you to be comfortable and at ease.

✔ **Listen to the complete question before answering** – if in doubt, ask for clarification.

✔ **Don't rely on your application form or CV to sell you.** No matter how qualified you are for the position, you will need to sell yourself in the interview on the day. Even if you work in the company, and know some of the interview board, you can't take it for granted that they know all about you. Sell yourself!

✔ **Keep your answers focused on the specific question** you are asked. Remember, the more you can talk about *yourself* and *your relevant skills,* the easier it will be for the interviewers to give you credit.

✔ **Be succinct and to the point** in your replies – any one answer shouldn't take more than a couple of minutes to deliver – remember, you will only have a specific amount of time allocated to you, so make sure every moment counts.

✔ **Try not to be afraid of quiet periods, pauses or drying up.** Interviewers appreciate how people feel in an interview situation. In many cases, they are nervous themselves. If you need a moment to compose yourself, take it. And don't forget to breathe – slowly. If there is water, take a drink, and if not, just ask for some.

✔ **Be honest** at all times – if you don't know something, say so.

Dressing to Impress

Dress as you would expect to dress if you had the job, or slightly better. If in doubt, err on the conservative side. This demonstrates respect to the interviewers and creates a good professional impression overall.

Here are some other very important points to help improve your personal presentation on the day.

General

• Beware of new clothes. New shoes might be painful during your interview, so best to break them in the week before. New shirts will have a strong crease across the chest area; best to wash and iron it before wearing it to interview.

- Make sure your clothes are comfortable and fit you well – particularly if you borrow something to wear.

> Recently, I had a candidate who was going for an interview with a large IT firm for their graduate programme. His suit looked like it needed a good ironing, if not a full dry-clean. Also, his suit jacket was clearly a size or two too small, straining on the arms and across the shoulders and back. So I asked him if that was the suit he was going to wear on the day.
>
> "Oh yes," he replied proudly, "that's the interview suit. Myself and the two other lads in the house pitched in and bought the suit between us last year. We brought it to London last summer, and it was great for the interviews . . ."

- Vertical stripes will make your body look longer and slimmer.
- Horizontal stripes will make your body look wider.
- Black, and other dark colours, will make you look slimmer.
- Light colours will make you look broader; ideal for someone who is trying to look heavier.
- Shoes are often taken as an indication of the person's attention to detail. Make sure they are clean and polished.
- Opt for a briefcase rather than a handbag or rucksack.
- Make sure your teeth are cleaned and that your breath is fresh – no garlic the night before.
- Ensure your hair (including beard and moustache) is well groomed.
- Use minimal cologne or perfume, but use a good deodorant. You don't want to be remembered for leaving a lingering heavy aroma of perfume, aftershave or, worse still, BO, which meant the room had to be aired before the next candidate.

Men

- Your suit should be wool, your shirt cotton, your tie silk and your shoes leather.

- Choose a conservative navy or grey suit, or other conservative colour such as black, beige or brown.
- Wear a white (or light-coloured) long-sleeved shirt with hard collar.
- If your suit and tie have patterns, tone down the look with a plain shirt. And if your suit and shirt are plain, brighten your look with a patterned tie.

Women

- Your suit, jewellery or accessories should not distract from your personality or what you're trying to say. Keep it simple. Avoid anything flashy i.e. handbags, shoes or jewellery.

- You can wear a wide variety of coloured suits and still be considered professional, but best to veer towards navy or grey, especially if you are going for a more senior position. Pastel jackets or shirts with bright floral designs do not look as professional as the traditional office suit.

- Keep make-up (and false tan) to a minimum, with lipstick and nail polish in conservative colours.

- Open shirts, v-necks and long necklaces all point to the cleavage. Decide beforehand if that is the effect you intend. Avoid clingy or tight tops.

- Likewise, if wearing a skirt suit make sure the skirt is not too short.

- Marks from make-up, fake tan or deodorants shouldn't be visible.

- Avoid using pins and tape will let you down when most needed.

- In general, earrings are fine but nothing too flashy or distracting. Any other piercing should be concealed. Avoid earrings that dangle and bracelets that might make noise on the table.

- Beware of light white linen skirts and trousers; they are often see-through.

Ask yourself: "Am I good enough to photograph?" If not, take corrective action. Ideally your look should be professional and classic. This does not mean you cannot be fashionable, though – once the suit you choose is professional, and not too "mother of the bride" or "ladies' day" at the races.

Handling Stress

Technically speaking, stress and nerves are a biochemical reaction to a perceived threat. The mind knows an important event is approaching and releases the chemical adrenaline to help you cope. Adrenaline does its job very well, which is why nerves are a good thing. The mind becomes sharper; the attention more focused. In other words, you will perform better *because* of nerves, not in spite of them.

That said, for some, nerves do present several unwelcome side-effects such as fear, thirst, irregular breathing, shakes, difficulty with food and sweating. In some cases you may even find it difficult to sleep the night beforehand, so get an early night, in case this happens. Here's my guide to surviving them all. But remember, if you prepare well for your interview, it's likely that you'll avoid them altogether.

Fear

In previous interviews, you may have felt nervous because you feared being asked questions that you hadn't prepared for. If you have gone through the proper preparation, this anxiety should pass quickly, because now you'll be working from your agenda and have prepared your answers to all the likely questions you'll be asked in any interview.

Furthermore, the interview panel expects you to be nervous, and allows for this. That's one of the reasons they start with relatively easy questions such as "What are the highlights of your CV?" which of course you will have prepared and rehearsed, so your nerves should pass in the first minute or two.

If you do go blank – say it. Tell the interviewers you've lost your train of thought and go back to the last main point you were making. If that's gone, ask them to repeat the question if necessary. Otherwise take a sip of water and wait for the next question.

Thirst

Adrenaline makes you thirsty, so drink plenty of water before and during the interview. And remember to take a trip to the loo immediately before the interview.

Avoid drinking alcohol or eating spicy food, or garlic the night before. Alcohol will reduce your ability to concentrate at the interview, and you'll be even thirstier. You also run the risk of still smelling of garlic or drink, which does not create the best impression.

Irregular breathing

To regulate your breathing, people will often suggest you take a deep breath. This may work, but sometimes it is better to exhale fully first to get rid of any lingering "used" air. Once deflated, your lungs will naturally re-inflate with fresh "good" air, giving your brain the oxygen it needs. Do this a few times in the minutes before the interview.

Shakes

To still your shaking hands, make tight fists with both your hands, and hold those fists as tight as you can for half a minute. Press your fingernails hard into the palms of your hands and watch the blood drain from your knuckles. Then relax your hands and straighten your fingers. The muscles of your hands will be too tired to shake for a long time, by which time hopefully you're on your third answer and well relaxed.

Difficulty with food

While you may not feel like eating on the morning of your interview, you should try to eat something light, and often. Sometimes nerves can shut down your digestive system and this could cause your blood sugar level to run low, and you won't be at your best for the interview. A banana is often a good food on such a day; a good source of energy, but not too demanding on your system. Avoid too much caffeine on the morning as this is a stimulant.

Sweating

We don't have a miracle cure for sweating except to suggest you invest in a really good deodorant so you stay dry for the interview. Avoid wearing tight or synthetic clothing which will only increase sweating. If you get sweaty palms, keep a tissue in your pocket and dry them just before you go into the interview room to shake hands.

If you are well prepared – know what you want to say; have practised saying it; and have carefully examined the job description and worked on the questions you are likely to be asked – then the potential difficulties you may have with nerves are likely to be reduced. Take a short walk outside in the fresh air to clear your head before the interview.

Chapter 7

Delivering Presentations and Other Selection Tools

Often there are a number of different stages in the selection process. These may involve other activities such as presentations, tests and assessment centres, to assess your skills and strengths in a variety of settings. In this chapter I'll cover a number of the alternative selection methods that organisations use to select staff. These include:

- Presentations at interview
- Assessment Centres

    1. Psychometric Tests – Aptitude Tests and Personality Tests
    2. Case Studies
    3. Presentations
    4. Group activities and discussions
    5. In-Tray Exercises

Making a Presentation at Interview

Sometimes you will be asked to prepare a presentation for the interview. Usually you will be asked to present at the start and then you'll be interviewed. Typical topics candidates are asked to present on include:

- ✔ What I will achieve during my first eighteen months
- ✔ My vision/business plan/priorities for the role of . . .
- ✔ My 100-day plan
- ✔ Challenges facing their industry and how their company can address them
- ✔ What I bring to the role
- ✔ Specific task in the role e.g. "My plan for introducing Performance Management" or "My plan for Business Development".

These are all areas that you should be preparing in advance of your interview anyway. Now you have the added advantage of having your material well structured and prepared in advance, and being able to present it at the start of the interview in a coherent way.

This gives you more control over the start of the interview. And this will give you the chance to get your plans and ideas for the job role (i.e. your agenda) on the table for discussion.

Preparing your Presentation

A presentation at an interview is no different from other presentations and the principles of good preparation and communication apply. Even if you are not used to giving presentations, here are the main steps you should follow to prepare fully. You need to be clear on the outcomes you want from the presentation – in this case to prove you are the best candidate for the role.

- **Know your audience** – the interview panel. Find out what you can about them in advance. Try to understand what their interest in the role might be. Your potential boss or the HR manager may be interested in different aspects, so pitch your presentation and delivery accordingly. You need to get them to listen to you. They will only listen to you for one of three reasons – if it **interests** them; if it **benefits** them or if it **affects** them.

- **Know what you want to say.** Identify the central theme of your presentation and make sure everything you say supports that – i.e., why you should get the job. Do not make sweeping general statements such as "my vision is to achieve best-in-class customer service" unless you can back them up with practical, specific and relevant action steps and plans. The interview board are interested in how you're going to deliver your vision or develop the business. Tell them.

- Use **illustrations, examples and pieces of evidence** that support the ideas you want to communicate. Provide examples from work and career achievements to demonstrate you have the track record and skills to deliver your vision and plan. Show how you will effectively use them to be successful in the role and contribute to their organisation.

- **Structure** your ideas into a logical sequence, from most important to least important. The sequence and flow of your presentation should make sense to the audience. There should be a clear beginning, middle (or number of middles) and ending. Don't overload your presentation. Remember, you are merely presenting your ideas and outlining your recommendations, in the hope that they will interest the interview board enough that they probe you more at the interview.

- **Rehearse** your presentation out loud a number of times until you have the flow. **Time** your presentation so you stay within the allocated time.

- **Prepare answers** for the questions you are likely to be asked. Anticipate the likely issues the interviewers will question you on and prepare the points you want to make. Use each answer to illustrate more points on your own agenda.

Using PowerPoint

You are likely to be offered a choice of using PowerPoint. PowerPoint is a great tool that has enhanced many presentations. However, it doesn't work if you simply use it as a crutch to deflect attention from yourself.

PowerPoint is especially useful for conveying visual material such as photographs, diagrams and organisational flowcharts. It loses its impact if the slides are crammed with text, and you end up reading them to your audience (in this case the interview panel).

If you decide to make your presentation using PowerPoint, here are some simple pointers:

Keep it simple:
- No more than one idea on each slide
- No more than four or five bullet points on each slide
- No more than one sentence in each bullet point

Less is more:
- Reduce paragraphs to sentences
- Reduce sentences to words

- Reduce words to pictures or graphics, where appropriate

- Use visuals and diagrams to illustrate your points rather than bullet points

- Keep colours simple – and do not use sound effects or imported cartoons

Using Flip Charts

If you are given the opportunity to use a flip chart, write up your flip charts in advance, so that your writing is clear and neat. The rules for PowerPoint also apply to flip charts: keep your charts simple; less is more. Practise delivering your charts.

One mistake presenters often make when using flip charts is that they try to write and present at the same time. Unfortunately, this means their back is towards the audience for too long, and they cannot be heard properly.

So prepare your flip chart pages in advance. Position the flip chart stand in a place from which you will be comfortable presenting, and where you can make good eye contact with your interviewers. Also, pre-prepared charts mean you don't make any spelling mistakes mid-presentation or find the marker drying up as you write.

Printed Handout/Report/Business plan

Working from a printed report or handout is another option for presentations at an interview. At Carr Communications, we usually advise that, rather than using PowerPoint or flip charts to deliver your presentation, you could prepare it in PowerPoint, and give the interviewers a printed copy of your presentation at the start.

However, there is the danger that the interviewers might look ahead and not really listen to you properly. So it is really important to keep them engaged and interested in each slide. Do this by talking them through it, using the handout as a working document during the presentation. This way your handout complements your presentation and reinforces your ideas and plans. Now they are focusing on you and what you will do in the job. This allows you to be much more engaging. Delivering your presentation in this manner also means that you can sit or stand, whichever you'd prefer – and you are not stuck to a podium controlling the projector.

Also, as appropriate, you can bring along props to support your presentation, e.g. a mock-up of a product design. If you are going for a role as a journalist, you might bring along some sample publications; or if you're seeking a construction project role, you could bring along a portfolio of building projects you have worked on.

Assessment Centres

An assessment centre is where a series of different selection methods, tests and activities are conducted, usually over a day. The exercises are designed to assess your abilities across a range of competencies in a number of exercises and situations, usually with a number of other candidates.

So what exactly are recruiters looking for at assessment centres?

✔ To see what you can do in a variety of situations

✔ Evidence of core competencies and skills

✔ To test your potential

✔ To see how you relate with other candidates, members of the organisation, and possibly your potential boss.

Typical assessment centre exercises include:

- Psychometric tests
    - Aptitude tests
    - Personality tests
- Case studies
- Giving presentations
- Group activities and discussions
- In-tray exercises

As in any test, remember to listen to and read instructions carefully. Write clearly, and ask for clarification if you don't understand.

1. Psychometric Tests

Psychometric tests are used to measure attributes like personality, intelligence and aptitude. Usually psychometric tests involve a series of multiple-choice questions that are designed to provide an insight into your reasoning abilities or how you would respond to different workplace situations, or how you could cope with the intellectual aspects of the role.

There are two main types of psychometric tests:

a) Aptitude Tests and **Ability Tests** are designed to assess your innate abilities and potential in skills such as verbal reasoning.

The purpose of an aptitude test is to assess your intellectual capacity in a range of areas including verbal comprehension, numeric ability, logical or analytical ability, and critical thinking or reasoning. The following shows a typical aptitude test question:

Consider the following series:

4, 5, 7, 10, 14,

What comes next?

A. 20   B. 16   C. 17   D. 18   E. 19

Answer: E   (4+1=5; 5+2 =7; 7+3=10; 10+4= 14; 14+5=19)

The main points to remember when doing aptitude tests:

- They are strictly timed under exam-like conditions
- Accuracy is more critical than speed
- You can skip questions you can't answer
- Usually multiple-choice exercises
- You can practise mock tests.

You'll find lots of sample aptitude tests on the internet, so try to get plenty of practice before the big day. It is also advisable to practise doing calculations without a calculator for those problem-solving and numerical tests.

b) Personality Tests and **Interest Inventories** are used to provide an indicator of your personality, your attitudes and work style against known personality traits.

These tests are useful for determining your fit with the culture of the organisation and your interests in certain areas. The outcomes of these tests may be used as the basis of the questions about your management style and motivation at the interview. The key points to remember about personality tests are:

- You must answer honestly

- They are usually not timed

- There are no right or wrong answers

- You can't practise

- Avoid guessing what they are looking for.

Again, you will find sample tests online which will give you a flavour of the type of questions you will encounter.

2. Case Studies

A case study can be an individual exercise or a group exercise. This can be followed by an individual interview or presentation, or a group discussion or a role-play on the content of the case study. Case studies are usually used to allow candidates to demonstrate their people skills and business skills.

For example, if the job in question is a management one, you might be given a brief telling you that you are in charge of a team of six people. Your task is to have a discussion with one of your team members because they haven't met their sales target in the previous six months.

You will also be given background information about the company, product and sales climate, and a file about the person you are about to meet.

You will be given sufficient time to prepare. Then you will play the manager while an actor plays the part of the underperforming salesperson. You will lead the meeting to achieve the objective outlined in the brief.

> During the role-play you'll need to demonstrate the relevant behaviours and approach to the meeting. For example, you'll need to show that you have the necessary skills: to provide feedback; to gain commitment to improvement and development from the staff members; to identify any issue or problems; and so on.

Often, this role-play scenario would be observed by two or more assessors in the room

Ultimately, the purpose of a case study exercise is to test your ability to:

- analyse information

- think clearly and logically

- make decisions based on the data provided

- present your analysis in a

  o one to one interview

  o a formal presentation to an interview panel

  o a group discussion with other candidates

  o role-play

These exercises are usually timed, allowing approximately fifteen to twenty minutes for preparation.

3. Presentations

Sometimes, you'll be asked to deliver a presentation as part of an assessment centre day. These may have a different emphasis to the presentations already discussed. At an assessment centre, they could be case study based and you are asked to present your findings, recommendations or plans based on a detailed information pack you will be given to read on the day. You'll be given ample time to read and digest the information and prepare your flip charts.

In some cases you will present to other candidates while in other cases you'll present directly to the assessors. You will be questioned in detail on your rationale for the decisions and recommendations you are making.

4. Group activities and discussions

The main objective of a group discussion is to see how you contribute to a team and interact with other people; how well you communicate with and influence others; how well you listen and take on others' ideas; and how well you make decisions and plan.

Group discussions may be centred on a general current affairs topic given on the day or a specific task using a case study. In a typical session, the group would be asked to discuss a topic such as "Why customer service is important"; or to plan an event, based on a given scenario and information provided.

Other group activities include:

- role-plays

- practical tasks, e.g. build something, make something (testing problem-solving skills, planning, creativity, ideas and team involvement).

5. In-Tray Exercises

In-tray exercises are exactly what their name states. They can be paper-based or online. Either way, your brief will be something like: "You are covering for Joe who's been away for a week and won't be back for some time. You are taking over his in-tray or email inbox until he returns."

So during a typical in-tray exercise, you will be given a bundle of "in-tray" post, memos and reminders, and asked to sort through and prioritise the inbox of an email account. Here, your organising, prioritising and planning skills are very important. Your speed and accuracy are also important, so it is important that you see the bigger picture and don't get bogged down in the detail.

The purpose of an in-tray exercise is to test your ability to:

- handle large volumes of information, both simple and complex

- use your judgement and prioritise responses

- organise and plan tasks and activities

- analyse data and information.

Based on the information in the in-tray, you may be asked to write a memo, write a task list with priorities or plan a meeting.

Chapter 8

Following the Interview

After the build up to the interview it can be easy to lose momentum, and in some cases just sit and wait. There are some important actions you can take after the interview so you are prepared for the next stages in the process and you learn from the previous stages.

These steps include:

- Debriefing after Interview
- Following up with Interviewers
- Preparing to Negotiate

Debriefing after Interview

As you leave an interview or assessment centre, your preparation for the next job interview or assessment should begin straight away. While your mind is still fresh, write down all the questions you were asked and the exercises you were given. Make a note of the question areas where you felt you did well and reflect on the reasons.

Also identify any items on your own agenda that you didn't get to discuss. Was that because you weren't asked? Or because you forgot to bring them up and mention them? You definitely won't forget these the next time round.

Reflect and think about any areas where you could have been better prepared and make a point of having your answers to those questions fully prepared for future interviews.

Following Up with Interviewers

Writing a follow-up email or letter to the interviewers following the interview is becoming more popular. And it certainly will make you stand out from the crowd.

You should have a clear purpose for writing the letter – thanking them for the opportunity to interview; re-visit an area from the interview you want to add to, or to make further recommendations or present ideas relevant to the role.

Whether you get the job or not, this is an opportunity to leave a lasting impression. Sometimes, the person who is offered the job turns it down, or might find after a couple of months that they're not the right fit. Who knows – you may well get another call.

Here's what that letter might say:

Dear Ms Reynolds,

I'd like to thank you and your panel for reviewing my suitability for the position of office administrator and giving me the opportunity to interview for the post.

I am, of course, very disappointed that I wasn't successful in getting the job, but I've no doubt you found an excellent person for the post.

I'd like you to know that I still feel that I would make a perfect match in your company in the role of office administrator. So, I would be grateful if you would keep my application on file and, should any other suitable vacancy arise, I'd love the opportunity to discuss how I could contribute to the administration department in your company.

Yours sincerely,

Anne O'Neill

Preparing to Negotiate

Congratulations, you've been offered the job! It's a great achievement, particularly in the current economic climate. However, your task is not complete yet.

Negotiating Salary

Try to avoid being the first to raise the issue of pay. When they raise it, find out the salary range they have in mind, and on what basis they decide where to put the new employee on that scale. This may often be known before the interview stage, e.g. from the ad or in preliminary research. In the public sector, the rules are usually tight, and someone with X experience goes in at a particular point in the salary scale, no matter how much you try to negotiate.

In the private sector, or in some other flexible systems, you'll need to be able to explain to your prospective employer why you believe you should be paid at a particular level. You will need to explain the value-add you bring to the job; what contribution you will make in the role, and link that to your salary.

Try to benchmark your salary expectations with similar roles in other organisations or sectors. Check with recruitment agencies and job websites for similar roles. Research current salary surveys for more insight into what you might reasonably expect to command in the current climate.

During negotiations, you will probably be asked about your current salary. Don't lie. They can easily deduce your salary in your previous job as soon as your tax information arrives in the payroll department for your new job. They won't take too kindly to finding you bumped up your salary by €10,000.

In the current economic climate, you can expect to be offered a salary up to 10–15% less than the salary you would have expected for the same role twelve to eighteen months ago. See if you can make up the balance with other benefits which are negotiable, such as annual leave, education support, performance bonus, travel or car allowance or a company car.

Negotiating Conditions

You should also get clarity around some of the practical terms and conditions of your employment. Ask questions about relevant issues such as:

• What do you expect from me in the first six months?

• How will my performance be measured?

• Who will I report to?

- How often can I expect to be away on business overnight?

- What will my office/facilities be like?

Even in today's difficult job market, it pays to be selective about what job you accept, and it's far easier to discuss the above topics before you accept the job, rather than after. Remember the earlier section on the components of your ideal job – this is where you clarify those issues.

Chapter 9

Seeking Graduate Roles

If you are fresh out of school or college, you should be filled with enthusiasm and confidence as you start off on your career path, aiming to find that ideal job.

However, many students I work with find themselves in a catch-22 situation – "I can't get work or experience because I don't have experience." This can be tricky to overcome. Also, you may not be sure exactly what you want to do at this stage in your career.

The current job market is more challenging than it has been in recent years, so you need to put your very best foot forward to succeed. And that means detailed preparation for each stage of the selection process.

Each chapter in this book will be relevant to your job search. However, in this part I have assembled all the information you are likely to require in your particular segment of the jobs market. I've arranged the information under the following headings:

- The Milk Round

- Social Evenings

- Career Services on Campus

- Not Knowing What You Want To Do

- Completing Graduate Application Forms

- Internships/Shadowing Programmes

- Assessment Centres and Group Interviews

- Dress to Impress on a Low Budget

- Making the Most of Little Experience

The Milk Round

The term "milk round" refers to the process of companies visiting third-level campuses around the country in a bid to attract the best and most talented potential employees. Typically, milk round employers are large corporations that offer structured graduate training programmes designed to give trainees practical experience in the various departments in the company over a period of years.

The milk round provides a great opportunity for you to network and to talk to some of the bigger recruiters in a range of industries, and find out how their graduate programme is run. To make the most of it, bear the following points in mind:

- **Be prepared.** Know which companies you are interested in. Do your research and know exactly what you want to ask each employer. Simply attending a career fair and wandering about aimlessly as you collect company brochures is not a valuable use of your time.

- **Look the part.** While a milk round event is not an interview, it represents your first opportunity to impress your target organisation, so why not dress in a way that reflects this?

Milk rounds on the web

In recent years and in the current economic climate, companies have increasingly transferred their milk round activity to the web. Many of the major firms reach out to a wide audience by providing detailed graduate programme information on their websites. This is a huge advantage if you attend a college that your target company does not usually visit.

There are other online resources available to you. **Gradireland.com** is a one-stop shop for any graduate embarking on a job search. In addition to listing vacancies, it provides a number of resources to aid you in your job search. Also check your own college website and the websites of other colleges in your area.

Social Evenings

Increasingly, potential employers invite students and graduates to social evenings in their offices or at a hotel. Senior people and current successful graduate trainees from the company speak about the various roles in the organisation and their work. These briefing evenings are very informative, giving you a real chance to talk to people in the firm and to learn about the work and opportunities available.

- Be well prepared in advance so you come away well informed, having spoken to the key people and having left a good impression.

- Ask intelligent questions of the senior management/partners and company representatives.

- Collect business cards and follow-up on conversations during the following week.

- Dress well.

- Drink little, if any, alcohol.

- Behave yourself.

Career Services on Campus

Often, the best and most underused service available to a student is the careers advisory service on their college campus. The members of staff there are professional advisors who have the experience, knowledge and links with potential employers to make a big difference in your job search. The services are usually up-to-date with market trends and where vacancies are to be found. And the service is free.

They will be able to point you in the direction of the roles you should be pursuing. In some of the colleges, the office will be equipped to provide psychometric tests, which may help you to understand what areas you might be interested in and what you would be best suited to.

Not Knowing What You Want To Do

So, you don't know what it is you want to do for the rest of your life. Don't worry. Very few twenty-somethings do know. Not many of your parents' generation knew either, but they still managed to build successful and focused careers.

No-one knows you better than you know yourself. So take some time out and do a little self-reflection. Go through the exercises in this book, particularly in Chapter 1, to help you clarify the following:

- What do I want to *do* every day at work?

- What are things people tell me I would be good at?

- What excites me?

- What are my personal values?

- What are the skills I have developed over the course of my studies?

Writing down the answers and reflecting on them may give you an insight into what you are good at and what you enjoy doing.

Do you have an inkling that accountancy may be your thing? Do you think a career as a commercial solicitor could be the one for you? Are you someone who could thrive in a PR environment? What about the hospitality industry? It is a good idea to dip your toe in as many sectors and organisations as possible, and gradually narrow down the options that interest and don't interest you.

And talk to people. Talk to people who were a few years ahead of you in college. Go to the talks that the college provides where people from some of the better-known companies provide an overview of life at that company.

I come across many young people who are diligent in filling out forms and assembling their CV. But they neglect to attend the talks given by people who work at their target companies and so are unprepared at interview, and in some cases actually don't know the type of organisation they are hoping to join. Fitting in with the organisation's culture is a critical aspect of job satisfaction. So do your research and talk to your tutors, last year's trainees and others to get an insight.

Completing Graduate Application Forms

In Chapter 3, I covered the practical steps and advice in relation to completing application forms. Graduate application forms are the same. However, here's some advice on completing graduate application forms from the HR Director of one of the "Big Five" accountancy firms.

> *Fill out forms completely and get them in on time. Some CVs and forms are now spellchecked online, so an application could be rejected even before it reaches the hands of a human being, particularly among the professional firms.*
>
> *And be very careful. I had the dubious pleasure of writing to a student to let him know that we had received his application form.*

> *Unfortunately for him, I was working in Accountancy Firm A, but he had sent us an application form for Accountancy Firm B. Needless to say, he didn't get a job with either firm. Professional firms need people who pay close attention to detail and he clearly wasn't that kind of person.*

Internships/Shadowing Programmes

Summer internships are a great way to gain an insight into potential career choices and at the same time enhance a CV that might otherwise show little "real" work experience. Getting summer work with an organisation is a great way to help you clarify what you might like to do in your career. You can apply for a summer job in the company or for a place on the summer internship programmes that many of the bigger firms run.

The internships (also known as shadowing programmes) run from four to twelve weeks. Bear in mind that getting a place on one of these programmes is a similar process to applying for a graduate position. You will need to put plenty of time and effort into your application and job interview.

You can expect to be treated as if you are there on a longer graduate trainee scheme. So put the head down, work hard during your internship, and you may just open the door to success further down the road, when the next year's graduate trainee scheme comes along.

Declan Farrell, one of our careers trainers, remembers one client who hadn't seen the importance of internships:

> I had a client who was looking for a legal traineeship. He had completed his initial degree and was taking time out before his legal exams and applying to firms at the same time. But he had a difficulty: although he had good exam results and was an otherwise good candidate, on his summer holidays he had not done any internships, so he had no way of showing that he had always been interested in law.
>
> There's a place on some of the forms that asks candidates to indicate when their interest in law arose. His lack of any internship or business/office experience made it difficult to suggest it was anything other than a sudden fancy.

> Internships usually involve junior work, and there is usually no offer of a job at the end of an internship, but we advise that you take them wherever and whenever possible.
>
> Having one or two internships on a CV is a sign to employers that you are serious and interested in this area and that you have taken the necessary steps towards starting a career in that area.

Recently, I met a student who saw her summer holidays during college as an opportunity to advance her career:

> She had a general business degree and dabbled in different areas. But most importantly, she took my advice on getting good general work experience.
>
> So, before leaving on her J1 to the USA, she lined up lowish-level admin work in a big accountancy firm in Manhattan, so she got good hands-on business experience. The following year she completed an internship with one of the big firms in Dublin, and during her final summer she worked in a call centre in one of the large financial services companies in the Leinster area. So by the time she graduated, she had gained good practical business skills: business acumen; commercial experience; and customer interaction experience. She is now able to sell herself as someone who has focused on her career, even if that focus wasn't all in one sector.

Assessment Centres and Group Interviews

As assessment centres often form part of graduate selection processes, I've included a short section here, but you'll find more information on assessment centres in Chapter 9. Assessment centres include a series of different selection methods and tests, which are designed to let you prove to your potential employer that you possess the range of skills and qualities necessary for the role you've applied for. Unlike a one-to-one interview, there will usually be a panel of several people assessing you and you will be assessed along with a number of other individuals – your competition.

Most assessment centres will include psychometric and aptitude tests, and business activities and tasks. These exercises are observed by a number of assessors who evaluate you on your competencies and qualities, your potential and how you relate to others.

A typical day at an assessment centre may look something like this:

9.00–9.30 a.m.	Briefing
9.30–11.00 a.m.	Aptitude tests
11.15–noon	Panel interview (incl. presentation)
1.30–3.30 p.m.	Case study exercises
4.00–4.45 p.m.	Group discussion

Assessment centre exercises may include:

- **In-tray Exercises** to test if you can handle large volumes of simple and complex information.

- **Group Discussions;** these are usually team tasks where assessors are looking for interpersonal skills such as influencing, team-working and leadership potential. Remember, you are not only competing against the other individuals in your group; you are competing with the standards of the organisation. Assertiveness is viewed positively, but arrogance and bad manners are not.

- **Role-plays;** these provide an opportunity for the assessors to see you "in action" – dealing with an irate client, negotiating a business deal, handling an underperforming staff member.

- **Presentations** are an opportunity to show your confidence in front of a group, with material that might be relevant to the job. Structure your information and communicate your points clearly to the appropriate audience.

- **Group Problem-Solving Exercises and Case Studies**; these exercises might involve a task or problem that the group has to work on together. Here, the prospective employer is looking for signs that the students have the ability to relate to other people, to communicate effectively and can work as part of a team to achieve a result. They are also looking to identify candidates who are organised, can manage their time and have leadership qualities, as well as the ability simply to complete their task.

Often tasks are strictly timed. Speed and accuracy are of the essence, so don't get bogged down on the detail, and avoid spending too long on each exercise. Remember, the assessment centre is designed to allow you to demonstrate your ability to do the job, not show up the areas where you're weak. However, it is a long day, so make sure to get your eight hours' sleep the night before.

Dressing to Impress (on a Budget)

Employers understand that students mightn't have the resources to afford the latest designer ensemble for the interview, but there is no excuse for worn, unkempt or dirty clothes. They expect that you'll be entering the workplace soon, so will want to see that you're at least capable of dressing in a professional manner.

Of course, if you're looking for work with Google or some other technology company, a more relaxed dress code will be acceptable when you are in the job. But for the interview, be conservative and wear the suit.

Even on a limited budget you can dress to impress. (See also the section Dressing to Impress, pages 78-80.)

Making the Most of Little Experience

Some graduates and students will have limited work-related experience, so you need to make the most of what you have. Don't write off anything as being "irrelevant"; instead, suggest ways to show that it is relevant.

Transferable skills are appropriately named as they can be used in any number of settings. If your only work experience is working in a bar on a part-time basis, use it in your CV to show the skills you gained (e.g. you work well in a customer-facing environment).

Similarly, participating in a group project in college demonstrates an ability to work in a team setting. And spending the summer waiting tables in the US may help you explain to an interview panel that you work well under pressure. Likewise, if you have voluntary and community work experience, highlight skills you developed such as fundraising, organising events, etc.

It has been said that experience is not what happens to you, it is what you do with what happens to you. So familiarise yourself with the skills required for the roles you are looking for and consider everything you have done that might demonstrate that you have these skills.

Chapter 10

Managing Redundancy

For many, the news that they are to lose their job will have a severe impact. You may feel shocked and upset. You may feel angry and depressed. However, even though these emotions are natural and appropriate to your circumstances, they can also be detrimental to your efforts to secure new employment.

The day you get word that your job is being terminated should be the same day that your new job search begins (if it hasn't already). It may be difficult, but it's important to remember not to take a redundancy personally. It is the job that is being made redundant, not the person. However, losing a job is a very personal experience. And you will go through all of the emotions that go with news of such a change to your circumstances.

Having worked with many individuals in this situation, this chapter provides personal insights and practical guidelines for helping you deal with the situation. Topics covered are:

- Shock, Upset and Anger

- Exit Interviews

- Mental Health

- Planning and Managing the Change

- Networking

Shock, Upset and Anger

The best place to express upset is among friends and family and far away from the workplace. You are unlikely to reverse your employer's decision, no matter how passionately you vent your anger, so it is best to accept it, be professional and give them the space and incentive to help you in your job search.

Strive for an amicable parting. See if they'll let you remain in situ for a few weeks, to begin your job search. The discipline of coming into a workplace every day will improve your morale and keep you focused on your next steps. This may not always be possible from a client confidentiality perspective. Some individuals I have worked with were told the news at lunchtime and were gone that evening. Again, this was connected with the level of confidential work they were responsible for.

Get a good reference in writing. If you can, ask that the reason for your departure be included on the reference. Something along the following lines: ". . . due to the downturn in our business, the role of customer services representative, along with a number of other roles, is now redundant . . ." This will also send a clear message to prospective employers that you were not at fault when your job was terminated.

Copper-fasten your reputation with a polite "thank-you" letter before you go. Your wording might go something like this:

Dear Helen,

I have finished all the paperwork and cleaned off my desk, but before I depart, I'd like to let you know that I'm grateful for the four years of challenges, learning opportunities and friendships that my position at XYZ provided for me.

I'd like to thank the board for hiring me at a time when I had so little experience and allowing me to grow and prosper in my several roles. I have no doubt that what I learned here will stand to me for many years to come.

I wish you and the company the very best of success.

Yours sincerely,

Mark.

Exit Interviews

These are part of the HR process and are very important from the company's perspective. This is where the company finds out how you rate your employment, and what they could have done better as your employer. Could the conditions have been better? Should more training have been made available? What do they need to know to avoid making mistakes when new people are hired in the years ahead?

This is an opportunity to give feedback in a constructive way, rather than a "behind the company's back" approach. It's an opportunity to get matters off the chest, but there is little benefit to a passionate vent. So keep it constructive.

Mental Health

Our jobs mean far more to us than just a salary. Our jobs often reflect our view of ourselves, our status in society, and – especially in men – will be linked to our self-esteem. When a job is lost, it is natural that some degree of despair follows.

At this time, it is important to remember your support network. Friends, family, medical practitioners and others are available and well positioned to help. Most people "don't like to interfere" so may be slow to offer assistance in case you'll be offended. But if you ask for their help, they are likely to excel in helping you get back on your feet.

This is not the time to cancel your gym membership, stop playing football with your friends or meeting the gang for drinks on Friday evenings. The money you save will have little overall effect on your current financial troubles, but losing touch with the people who can help you will.

You need to be strong and cheerful for the often difficult campaign that lies ahead as you start planning and managing your career transition. You will not be that person if you have spent the weeks before an interview sitting at home alone, worrying about your situation. So, chin up, chest out and have a spring in your step.

And learn from one of our clients, Donald, who outlines his story below:

My redundancy happened very quickly. One week, I was doing my typical fifty hours, and the following week, I had nowhere to go.

The first few days, I was full of energy and motivation. I sent off a load of CVs and letters. But after a while, my motivation ebbed.

I noticed it was harder to get up every morning. I was going to bed later and sleeping later, until soon I was sleeping until noon and eating my breakfast while watching the afternoon soaps.

I no longer shaved every day, and started wearing "comfortable" clothes that were ideal for moping around the house, but not for meeting people. I didn't keep up some of my friendships because I felt I couldn't afford to.

All of this reflected in a string of unsuccessful interviews. It is difficult to appear confident and competent if you're not feeling that inside.

It took many weeks before I realised I was in a downward spiral towards indifference and depression. It was clear that if I didn't soon take control, I could find myself in even greater difficulty.

I decided to set myself the same sleeping routine that I had had when I was employed. Even though I had no job to get up for, I still got up early, showered, shaved and put on a fresh shirt. I made sure to start my job search at the same time every day, and set a modest target of three job applications per week. Most importantly, I made a point of meeting a friend or professional contact for lunch or coffee three days a week. I put aside money for this, but you'd be surprised at how many people insist on picking up the tab when they hear you've been laid off. All this was good for contacts and my morale.

Of course, it didn't yield a job straight away, but it put me in the right frame of mind to compete for one. It took a few months, but eventually things worked out well for me.

The most important factor was the decision to stop moping and take control. When I had the discipline to start every day properly, I felt stronger and happier.

Planning and Managing the Change

Sometimes people react to a lay-off with a surge of defiant energy that sees them sending out CVs and cover letters by the dozen each week. Although this approach can have its benefits, remember that it is the quality of your applications – not the quantity – that matters. It is better to approach your lay-off in a structured way, and don't attempt to rectify your situation too quickly.

Take the considered and structured approach that is discussed in Chapter 1, "Evaluating your Career". One client of ours, Clodagh, approached her job search this way and found clear and long-lasting benefits. She had known several months in advance that she would be laid off, so she started on a course of career planning and coaching, eight weeks before she was officially terminated. She says:

By planning for my departure I had the opportunity to look back at my career to examine what had gone well and what hadn't. It was a very interesting journey.

It was useful for me to be reminded of what a good job I had done in some areas of my career. In normal life, we aren't reminded often of the things we do well, but by conducting this review I was able to accept my achievements and this boosted my confidence.

Because I also needed to collect references, I reconnected with some of the key people I had worked with during my fourteen years in the organisation. There was a lot of reminiscing over old times, and in all cases I got a firm commitment of help from colleagues. All of the people I contacted were true to their word; some with just a reference, others with leads for jobs.

The remarkable thing was that the process of being laid off, which should have been a completely negative and upsetting experience, turned out to be a pleasant one. Yes, I still lost my job, but my confidence was boosted in other ways. For the first time in my life, I sat down to consider exactly what kind of career I wanted.

It was then I realised that I wanted to change industry. If I hadn't worked through the full career change process and really evaluated my career and skills, and considered where I wanted to be, I could easily have just applied for a similar job to the one I'd left. Now, I have a new job, in a new and more exciting industry that I'm getting a buzz from, because I knew how my transferable skills and experience would fit in.

Networking

There are several lessons to be learned from Clodagh's experience above, and one of those relates to networking with previous colleagues and contacts. Irish people often instinctively keep bad news to themselves. They may not tell people that they have lost their job. They might feel embarrassed or fear that they will be viewed as responsible for the loss.

However, building up your network of business and personal contacts and informing them of your situation may prove invaluable in getting you an early meeting or interview with someone who may be able to "point you in the right direction".

Another client, Sarah, seemed to embrace all of the approaches we suggest when she got laid off. Here, she recalls how her system worked for her:

When I got laid off I experienced a range of emotions that included anger, despair and bewilderment. I wasn't last in, so why was I one of the first out when the company started going through a tough patch?

However, I said nothing, and the company softened the blow somewhat by allowing me to remain at my desk using their facilities until I got a new job. This had benefits beyond what was initially intended.

First of all, I kept my routine. I kept regular office hours, and kept up lunch routines with my former colleagues. This kept my morale high.

However, the real benefits were to follow when I got called to interview. The job required a degree of technical knowledge, so I went across the hall to the IT expert in our office, and he gave me a great overview of the systems and areas. I'd need to focus on for the interview.

I also spoke to one of our directors who was able to give me a good steer on my prospective employers. And I spoke to our HR person, who gave me a dry-run interview that was every bit as challenging as the real one.

On top of all this, I had plenty of time to prepare for the interview. I spent four full days reading reports about the company, its competitors, and the regulatory environment in which they operated. I had never spent so much time – and so much quality time – preparing for an interview. And I got interview coaching. For the first time in my life, I had prepared properly for an interview.

Needless to say, I was brilliant. If I say so myself. There wasn't a question that I hadn't predicted, nor an example I neglected to use. I showed a deep and wide understanding of the role.

I was called to a second interview. Once again I sat with several people in the company who helped me prepare, and I also met with external people who had comparable positions to the one I was seeking. I spent three days preparing – so a total of seven days' preparation for the two interviews. This was approximately fourteen times more preparation than I had ever put in for any previous position.

I was successful. I now have a senior position in a strong organisation. I'm very, very lucky. But I also wonder about all the jobs that I have applied for unsuccessfully down the years. All those opportunities missed because of a slapdash approach to job seeking. Next time I'm back on the job market, I intend committing the same time and effort towards my interviews.

And Finally...

Now that I have taken you through all the stages of career change, from preparing to look for jobs through to finding and getting the job you want, the next step is to get started, if you haven't already.

As you do, remember your attitude and motivation will determine how effective you'll be at each stage in the process. So make sure you keep focused and have a daily "to-do list" to keep you on track. Apply and use the many practical techniques described throughout the book that have worked for others – developing a useful network; being organised; keeping the job search broad; preparing fully in advance of interviews and learning from each one.

Reflect frequently on your effectiveness at the various stages in the job hunting process. Identify what is working for you and what isn't. Seek feedback and assistance – from interviewers, agencies, your network and others who will give you a good steer. Listen and change your approach if necessary or appropriate.

I've stressed the importance of being prepared as you plan and manage your career change. Louis Pasteur's words, "Chance favours the prepared mind", are equally true in this context. You need to be ready to act when opportunities arise – so be prepared.

I wish you the very best of luck with your preparation, and I hope this book has helped you to navigate your way through your career change and to *Find that Job.*

Free postage *
Worldwide

on our web site
www.poolbeg.com

Direct to your home!

If you enjoyed this book why not visit our web site

and get another book delivered straight to your home or to a friend's home!

www.poolbeg.com

All orders are despatched within 24 hours

* See web site for details

Carr Communications

www.carrcommunications.ie

www.poolbeg.com